WHAT TO PLAY—
WHAT TO TEACH

AN ANNOTATED OUTLINE OF THE PIANO-
FORTE MATERIAL ARRANGED IN
PROGRAMME FORM FROM THE
FIRST BEGINNINGS TO THE
WORK OF THE GREAT
PIANISTS

BY

HARRIETTE BROWER

AUTHOR OF
"Piano Mastery," "Vocal Mastery," "Life Stories of Master Musicians,"
"Self Help in Piano Study"

THEO. PRESSER CO.
PHILADELPHIA, PA.

CONTENTS

PART ONE

PART TWO

CONTENTS vii

PART THREE

PART FOUR

PART FIVE

PRELUDE

The following studies in the Selection of Study and Teaching Material and in The Art of Programme Building are the result of long patient effort, and many years of experiment and experience, years of studying the subject from all possible angles, while planning both personal programmes and those for students.

The art of programme formation is a neglected art. As yet it has received very little notice or cultivation. This is the first attempt to suggest building plans, or to hint that such are needed.

However, the subject is a fascinating one, and, if space were no consideration, a few paragraphs from each of the great players might have been secured. A few artists have made suggestions, from which the thoughtful player and teacher may glean help and inspiration.

Planning youthful programmes, with suggestions for study of the pieces named, is a feature. Also the careful consideration of artist programmes taken from each season's output. Programmes from various music schools, with comments of the directors, will be of interest. Lastly we are permitted to glance into the piano classes of two master teachers, Cortot and Schmitz.

Altogether we hope there will be food for thought along all these lines for the serious teacher and artistic pianist.

HARRIETTE BROWER.

WHAT TO PLAY—
WHAT TO TEACH

CHAPTER I

In "Self Help in Piano Study," the author developed the technical side of piano playing, from the foundation up. It was carefully explained just what to do at the very beginning, how to form the hand, how to shape the fingers, how to acquire correct physical conditions. It was shown from the start how to move the fingers with precision and accuracy.

From these beginnings the student advanced step by step, from the use of one finger to pairs, then through the five fingers consecutively. Still advancing, he practiced the Trill, Chords, Scales, Arpeggios and Octaves. He also acquired a variety of touches, to be used with various degrees of power and delicacy. These acquisitions and the processes by which they were gained, should be mentally reviewed by the student with faithful persistency, to keep them constantly in mind. A player too often makes the serious mistake of neglecting the beginning in his haste to advance and reach the goal. For this reason we shall occasionally recall the earlier steps, lest we forget what has been gone over, and the means by which we have reached our present degree of facility. For not one of the foundation principles stated in the little work mentioned, is to be cast aside. If it was worth learning once, it is worth retaining as a working principle to promote the object we are pursuing—mastery of the piano and its literature.

After learning the main technical principles underlying tone production on the piano, we began to apply them in mastering first an étude, then a piece. All exercises were memorized, the work of memorizing being practically explained and demonstrated.

THE GARDEN OF TONES

Having advanced from these early stages, we now find ourselves, as it were, at the portals of a vast Garden of Tones. Here are blooming flowers of every shape, size and hue. With the preliminary training already acquired, we are free to enter this Tone Garden and gather of its abundance. But, like children, we may pluck the things that do not profit, or others we shall be obliged to cast away for lack of ability to hold them.

In order to guide young teachers or self-taught students, we propose to plan some programmes, beginning with the earlier stages and advancing by degrees to higher levels.

ARRANGEMENT

To arrange a programme of piano music and to perform it at all adequately seems, to the young student, a very great undertaking indeed. In truth he seldom thinks of accomplishing such a feat, at least not until he has studied quite a number of years. Perhaps he never thinks of such a thing as a programme at all, but merely wanders here and there through the Garden of Tones, aimlessly culling whatever blossoms claim his attention. With the aid of a guiding hand, with suggestions as to selection, interpretation and performance, he would naturally work more systematically and successfully.

How often do we hear the remark: Such and such an artist played well, but had a badly arranged programme. One would suppose a good artist would be quite able to plan a list of compositions which would work out well, yet we must admit such is not always the case. Pianists often err in putting too many long, heavy works before an audience. Even the greatest artists are guilty of this error. When they have done so they should not be surprised when many of the audience leave the hall. This act, which seems to ardent music lovers so disrespectful and which we all deplore, is sometimes simply a silent protest against a too heavy, lengthy programme. When Von Bülow played the last five sonatas of Beethoven, or Josef Hofmann the *Sonata Op. 106,* together with a number of other very long compositions, neither the high scholarship and mastery of the one nor the consummate interpretative gifts of the other, could detain those who grew restive.

SOME REQUISITES FOR PROGRAMME BUILDING

What then are some of the requisites for a successfully arranged programme? Some of the following points should be considered.

First: Variety of style among pieces selected.

Second: Length of time required for performance.

Third: Contrast of keys.

Fourth: Variety of content in pieces.

Fifth: Perfect Mastery of every composition.

1. Variety of Style. A great deal is written against what is termed a "regulation programme." By this is usually meant a programme that begins with Bach and ends with Liszt. Critics must listen to many programmes during the season; for this reason, doubtless, they tire of those made up on these lines. To the student and young player, however, such an arrangement is of much value. It gives briefly a taste of the different styles of composition from the classic to the modern; it is an epitome of the growth and development of the art of piano playing; it gives a general glance over the field of piano literature. Such a programme complies with the first element of programme interest— variety.

But it need not follow that because we begin our programme with the universal master Bach, we must therefore add Mozart, Beethoven and so on down to Liszt, for we may wish to contrast some moderns with Bach, and not include any Beethoven or even Liszt at all. Nevertheless, it gives the player a certain sense of satisfaction and contentment to begin with one or more classical selections; just as we place the substantial part of our daily repast first and finish with sweets. There are people who are freakish enough to begin at the other end, with sweets, and work backward, but they are comparatively few.

If there is to be one long selection—say a sonata —on your programme, it need not be placed at the very beginning, no matter how much you may wish to have it over with and out of the way. Lead up to it through a group of shorter pieces. For this reason some of the shorter pieces of Bach, Scarlatti or other older masters are very useful to start with.

Then, too, we must become educated out of the belief that classical music, so called, is dry and soulless. When rightly selected and well played, it should be, and is, of great variety and charm. In reality it is never dry, dull or gloomy, but apt to be full of sprightly gaiety, though naturally there are some shadows to contrast with the sunlight. There is always plenty of melody, if we only know how to find these melodies. Let us ever bear in mind that composers of a century or two ago were as human as those of today; they had the same loves and hopes, the same sorrows and aspirations. It is to be granted they had other ways of expressing these feelings from the ways of moderns. But when we study into their idioms and ways of thought, we find their music palpitates with feeling—indeed with every possible variety of emotion.

So then, it is our duty—our privilege, to learn the meaning of all styles, both classic and modern, to find in each the feeling and emotion that lie hidden behind the notes. Those black marks on the paper are merely the signs and symbols of feelings which clamored for tonal expression. Bach was the colossal genius who expressed every shade of thought and emotion—in his own manner, of course. Scarlatti, Mozart, Haydn, Mendelssohn, Schubert, Schumann, Chopin and Liszt set down their thoughts in the way and manner individual to them. We call this particular manner their style. Each composer who has anything of value to express in his music, has his own particular style or way of saying it. It is through a mingling of various styles on a programme that we secure that desired variety which bars monotony.

ONE COMPOSER PROGRAMMES

It is true that an artist sometimes plays a programme which contains only the music of one composer. First of all the composer is generally one of the greatest. Second, his music probably has great variety of content if not always of style. Third, the performer's art should be superlatively great, to prevent the monotony felt inevitably in the performance of a less skillful player, under like circumstances.

II.   LENGTH OF TIME REQUIRED

II.   The second requisite for a successful programme is length of time required for the whole performance, also length of each composition. A very long programme is never desirable, no matter how noble the music, or how beautifully it is performed, because it taxes too severely the patience of the listeners. The best arrangement of pieces which may appear on paper, may be unsuccessful before an audience, for the simple reason that it is much too long. Especially is this true with regard to student programmes. Inexperienced teachers place each of their pupils two or three times on the programme; the result is a nightmare to the audience, especially if it has to listen to several sonatas! We advise these over-zealous teachers not to expect people to sit through the length of a whole sonata on such occasions. Cut your programme in half and make two performances of it. Artists and managers are learning the musical and artistic value of shorter concert programmes. Sometimes an artist may present but two or three compositions; but they will be so contrasted and of such diverse styles that the result is satisfying and complete.

A suggestion might be made here in regard to choosing selections appropriate to time, place and occasion. For instance, do not inflict a long, serious composition on guests at a social function. The other evening we were present when one of these inartistic mistakes happened. A teacher brought a pupil of hers to entertain guests at a large reception tendered two prominent musical educators, and attended by many pianists and musicians. When music was requested, a pretty young girl seated herself at the piano, and all expected something pleasing and suitable for the occasion. Dismay spread over many faces when the girl began a Beethoven sonata. She got through the first movement without any serious mishap, and rose from the instrument. Mistaking friendly applause for desire to hear more of the same sort, her teacher sent her back to finish the whole work! What the musicians present suffered in that last quarter of an hour need not be told. But one can also learn from unpleasant experiences. This episode taught the writer never, never to allow a Beethoven sonata at an evening company, where the music of Liszt, Moszkowski, Rubinstein or MacDowell would delight the listeners.

III.   VARIETY OF KEYS

III.   This is a point often overlooked when arranging a programme.   An ear sensitive to musical sounds and effects is oppressed with monotony when listening to several pieces in succession written in the same tonality, though perhaps without knowing the reason.   Not only should there be variety in tonality but the interchange of major and minor modes should be considered.   A most casual glance through the works of the masters proves this fact. With what care does Beethoven provide for this variety of keys and modes in his sonatas and variations.   The same principle applies to a group of pieces in which a common key predominates.   This difficulty can be easily obviated by taking thought.

IV.   VARIETY OF CONTENT

IV.   As we well know, music can be sad or gay, boisterous or quiet, chivalrous, humorous or exalted; indeed it can express these and a hundred other emotions.   Therefore, in making up our programmes we do not gather all of one kind and all of another; not all pieces in major keys, which express gaiety, and all sad pieces in minor keys; we rather contrast them according to their content. Again it can be affirmed that perhaps the whole secret of arranging an interesting programme is the idea of contrast.   Schumann understood this principle when he gathered those charming tone pictures in many moods together and called them "Papillons," "Carneval," "Faschingsschwank," and so on. The critics said he could not write in sustained style, but must join many short pieces together in order to make a long one. Suppose he did so—what then? We are the gainers, for these groups of short pieces are full of variety and never weary the listener. It is the same with MacDowell. What exquisite variety of content is found in his "Woodland Sketches," "Sea Pieces," "Marionettes," and other groups. Grieg is another composer who contrasts his short pieces in groups, expressing many moods. This very fact suggests the contrast and variety of content so necessary to sustain interest.

V.   PERFECT MASTERY OF THE COMPOSITION

V.   There is an oft-repeated saying: "It matters not so much *what* you play as *how* you play it." Consummate mastery of the composition goes far to make even an ill-arranged programme acceptable; when applied to an artistically planned list, mastery provides moments of supreme delight to the appreciative listener.

The *how* is the kernel of the whole matter, and this is what shall principally concern us in the studies which follow. The carefully planned programme is void of interest if indifferently performed. If the pieces are beyond the technical and intellectual capabilities of the player, there can be no adequate interpretation. And this is the great blemish of a large per cent of the semi-professional performance one hears. First the technic is undeveloped and thus power and velocity are lacking. When these are present there may be "too much technic and not enough soul." A well-balanced performance of even simple music gives true satisfaction.

The ideal programme, well arranged and performed with taste and understanding, holds interest from first note to the last, and makes a convincing appeal. It contains just the right number of pieces of contrasted length, style and content. It has sufficient variety to prevent monotony, yet not so much of constant change that we grow restless in the hearing.

The truly satisfying programme is one which contains some familiar and well-known works as well as some novelties. When only new works are presented the audience usually disapproves. A mingling of both old and new is the better way.

It goes without saying that before we can build the simplest programme, we must be able to perform several pieces straight through from beginning to end without errors or stumbling. When we can play these selections with absolute correctness from first note to the last, we are ready for the finishing touches, the refinements of style, the nuances, the intimate shadings which will render them truly artistic. A simple piece may be rendered unique by the manner in which it is performed.   We shall start with quite easy numbers and advance to more and more ambitious pieces.   The aim of our programme building is not only to indicate a choice of pieces and how they may be grouped, but to aid in their artistic interpretation.

CHAPTER II

A FIRST PROGRAMME

After the foregoing talk, in which we considered
some of the elements which enter into the making
of an acceptable programme of piano music, we will
begin to build some progressive programmes whose
object may be to incite the learner to systematic
study of pieces. The one first suggested is quite
simple, and is to be used by the student who has had
but a limited period of study. It is designed to follow the lessons in technic already referred to and
to supplement them through the application of the
principles of tone production for chord, scale, arpeggio, trills and octaves, which have been carefully
explained. And not only are technical principles
to be applied to these little pieces, but also the deeper
considerations of poise and repose, so necessary
for an artistic interpretation. For the student cannot too early attempt to realize that music is an art
requiring the active co-operation of mental and
physical powers, and is at the same time a medium
of emotional expression.

This first programme exemplifies a variety of
styles, both classic and modern. It will be sound
sense to begin with Bach, as the study of his music

is "an education in itself, for a knowledge of Bach creates a love for Bach," which is something we all have need of. Let us first consider the following list:

PROGRAMME ONE

Bach, *Two Minuettes in G;* Mozart, *Variations in C;* Schumann, Group from "Album for the Young, Op. 68"; Lange, *Beetle's Buzz;* Heller, (a) *Curious Story,* (b) *Little Tarantelle;* Grieg, Group from Op. 12; Reinhold, *Hungarian Battle Song.*

Bach. These little Minuettes, with which we begin, are dainty dances, taken from the "Piano Book" which the composer wrote for his second wife, Anna Magdalena. She was a young girl of twenty-one, and Bach was thirty-six when they were married. It was indeed a pleasure to him to instruct his young bride in the art of playing on the clavichord. Bach has left a goodly number of charming little pieces, which give teaching material of the highest value. Some of these small pieces have been gathered into two booklets, edited by Walter Carroll. MacDowell has also edited a set of the same pieces. The student can study these minuettes from either source; MacDowell's will be found somewhat more difficult.

Mr. Carroll says in his preface, "Each little piece should pass through three stages of preparation: A, Accuracy of notes, time and fingering; B, closer attention to phrasing, expression and speed; C, performance from memory. Whether these pieces be used as studies or pieces is immaterial, as they combine the technical value of the one with the grace and charm of the other. The elements of truth, sincerity and refinement are revealed in every bar of the music; elements at once the source of his greatness and the measure of his power."

From the above is seen what we must look out for in the study of the simplest Bach music, namely, accuracy of notes, time, fingering and phrasing. All these should occupy the student in the study of any piece whatever. Furthermore, if we attend at once to the memorizing, taking two or four measures at a time, we shall not be obliged to wait till we have come to the end of the piece before beginning to memorize it; we shall learn it as we go along. Then there will only be the working up for *tempo*, tone color, expression and finish.

The first *Minuette, No. 1* in the Carroll edition, is in G major. Recite the scale up and back, also triads of the key, as preparation for study of the piece. It consists of two parts of sixteen measures each. The melody is in the right hand, though once in awhile a little counter figure answers in the left hand. Make the pretty theme *sing,* with clean, pure tone; the detached tones can be played with combined arm and hand movement, with firm or elastic fingers. This little piece should be interpreted in simple, unaffected style, observing each note and mark of expression in its proper place.

The second *Minuette* (No. 3 in this edition) is also in the key of G. It is a study in arpeggio, that is, broken tonic chords. Though still simple in design it is a trifle more extended than the other. Care must be taken not to hold down all the keys of the broken chord at once, nor to overlap them in any way. There is something sonorous and imposing about this little minuette; indeed it has been arranged for full orchestra, in which form it is very effective.

Mozart. When it is asked what to play or teach of Mozart in simple form, let us not overlook this familiar *Theme with Variations*. They are indeed simple, but lovely in effect. The Theme itself is an old nursery folk tune; it gives opportunity for the melody touch, produced with fingers a little flattened and the arm weight we have dwelt on so frequently. As the Theme rises and falls, let the tone increase and diminish also. When the player can perform this seemingly simple piece from memory, without a slip, with beautiful quality of tone, good shading and phrasing, he may be well pleased with his progress.

Schumann. Schumann must have loved children with sincere affection to have written so many pieces for them and about them. He himself was simple as a child, a fact in itself the test of true greatness. The set of pieces comprised in the "Album for the Young, Op. 68," are forty-three in number, and every pianist should know and love them. When a great pianist, like Harold Bauer, performs them entire in recital, their perennial beauty comes home to us with a new and compelling force.

Let us study No. 10, the *Merry Peasant,* or *Happy Farmer.* Here we have the germ form of all lyric music, the melody in one hand, the accompaniment in the other. Contrary to what we have yet met with, the melody is here in the left hand. It must be made prominent, while the chords in right hand are subdued. The tendency is usually to play right hand too loud, and to hold down the second chord of the pair. This is not allowable, and care must be taken to play the chords lightly, with *marcato* touch, using combined wrist and arm movements.

In another style is the *Wild Horseman,* Number 8. Here the melody is in the right hand, the chords in the left. Play the *staccatos* with plastic fingers, with correct phrasing and accents; the left hand with rotary chord movements. After the double bar, throughout the middle section, which is in F major, the theme is found in left hand. It is here more difficult to bring out, owing to the quick tempo. After this the first period in A minor returns and closes the piece. Thus the *Wild Horseman* contains three perfect periods of eight measures each, the first and last being in A minor.

Among the many little gems of this set, each voicing a sweet or tender thought, we may choose Number 11, for melody and phrasing. It is called a *Sicilienne* and has a rocking kind of melody in 6/8 rhythm. Correct touch and phrasing are necessary to make this little piece expressive. The middle section needs clean, clear finger action, with detached, rebounding touch and careful attention to accents. The left hand chords must be well prepared by the fingers and played with arm weight.

Gustav Lange. The *"Beetle's Buzz"* was recommended to me years ago by a successful pedagogue, as "about the dearest little piece in the world." Simple as it seems, I have seldom found a young player able to make the trills in the right hand "buzz" with anything like the necessary smoothness and clarity, unless she had been drilled in the fundamentals as laid down in our technic study. Play the trills with distinct finger action and quiet hand, the melody sections with a singing tone. A light detached touch for the trills will be found very effective, and can be used with little effort.

Stephen Heller. When we come to the name of Stephen Heller, we find a composer who wrote only for the piano and in the romantic manner. Schumann praised his music, which has so much grace, fluency and variety of thought. He wrote many sets of studies and pieces, which have always been popular with students.

The *Curious Story* seems to relate a real narrative. Always use the second finger before the first at the beginning of the triplet figure, throughout the piece. In the middle of second part comes a halt in the story, where we find a few measures of deeper meaning, to be played slowly, reflectively, with expressive tone. The *Coda* is made up of the two chords. Analyze them, together with the fingering, before playing them. If this is done the passage is already memorized. Of course the whole piece should be played by heart, for only so can it be delivered with sufficient abandon. It is full of expressive variety and charm.

The *Little Tarantelle,* so named to distinguish it from the larger *Tarantelle in A flat,* is an excellent study in the velocity of simple figures, and forms a companion to the *Curious Story.* Study it slowly and memorize; then work it up with metronome from slow to quick *tempo.*

Grieg. With Grieg we come to a great modern romantic spirit. Here we find folk melodies used as a basis for many of his pieces. Grieg, like Schumann and MacDowell, wrote in the smaller forms, and each of his pieces, even the smallest, is the expression of a picture or mood, and is artistically molded and finished. The style will appear to be quite different from the style of the other composers on our list; but familiarity with Grieg's harmonies and manner of writing will teach us to see their many beauties. The harmonies which appear strange or even a bit harsh at first, will soften and grow mellow with better knowledge of them, while the melodies which seemed at the outset rather bizarre and unusual, will become well-liked, because we are better able to comprehend them.

Grieg wrote nearly a score of booklets, containing about half a dozen pieces each. Among these perhaps the set, Op. 12, is the simplest.

Let us look at the first one of the set. An *Aria,* therefore a song. Notice the key—E Flat—and recite its chords. Play the melody by itself till you know it, then add the accompanying sixteenths. Learn to sing the melody with the fingers, while playing the subdued notes that go with it. The left hand has the bass or foundation tone, besides the others which it must play. These sixteenth notes must sound as though played with one hand, so smooth and connected should they be. Yet we must keep them so subdued that the melody can sound above them. This little piece is an especially good study for the thumbs. They must not hold their keys an instant beyond the allotted time, or the tones will sound too loud and overbalance the other tones of the accompaniment. An expressive example of the lyric, singing style.

A pretty companion to the *Arietta* is the following *Valse,* in A minor. Note the rhythmic character of the bass. The first note has an accent; it is played with the down-arm movement and arm weight. This weight is carried over to the second beat, at which the hand and arm are raised, thus lifting the fingers off the keys. The melody in right hand must be exact in rhythm and well

phrased. The A major section especially is filled
with the spirit of the Northland; indeed the whole
piece reflects the originality and felicity of the
composer. Another caution is to make the melody
very rhythmic and exact in time all through. Use
metronome when studying it.

Passing over the intervening pieces, the *Album
Leaf* may be chosen to add to the others. Here the
same care must be given to the bass, to connect the
single note each time with the chord. Turn the
hand at the wrist to accomplish this. It will be
seen the melody is part of the time in the right hand
and part of the time in bass. It must always stand
out above the accompaniment.

Hugo Reinhold. Reinhold is the author of the
stirring little piece called *A Hungarian Battle Song*.
Its phrases and melodies are very descriptive. We
need firm, decisive touch, exact rhythm and accents. The brief passage on second page in slower
tempo, is in the nature of a prayer before the coming conflict. It is to be played with expressive
touch.

All of the above selections should be memorized
and performed without slip or hesitation. A simple piece, played beautifully, is a joy to listen to.

And never forget—it is not so much *what* you
play as *how* you play it.

CHAPTER III

PROGRAMME NUMBER TWO

J. S. Bach, *Gavotte and Musette,* G minor; Mozart, *Fantaisie,* D minor; Beethoven, *Bagatelle,* Op. 33, No. 1; Mendelssohn, *Songs without Words,* Nos. 6 and 45; Chopin, *Preludes,* 1, 3, 7, 10, 20; Leschetizky, *The Two Larks.*

As we have already noted, there are groups of delightful dances and other short pieces, by grand old Sebastian Bach, with which every student and music lover should be familiar. These pieces have been collected by different editors and the selections as well as the marks vary. My group was issued by Litolff, Number 386; it is an old and battered copy but beloved and now difficult to obtain. I turn the leaves affectionately, for each piece is a gem. Some of them have been marked and annotated by the hand of artists since passed away; William H. Sherwood among the rest.

The first number in this collection is the *Gavotte and Musette* we are about to study. The *Gavotte* is a charming little piece, brimming with gaiety and life. Its rhythm is very incisive and must be brought out with crisp accents. A gavotte, you know, is one of the old French dance forms, and it always begins on the second half of the measure.

The first two measures here are *forte,* while the following two are *piano.* The piece abounds in these contrasts, though some pianists, among them Harold Bauer, prefer to play it *mezzo* in tone all through. At the double bar, Sherwood advised a long instead of a short appoggiatura, as written. I also prefer it. At the ninth measure comes the working out of the theme. Here are accents again, with clear, firm *legato* or *marcato* touch, as the case may be. At the fifteenth measure the theme appears in bass, with trill in right hand. Play trill in sixteenth notes and make theme stand well out above it. In the left hand trill which follows, use A flat as the auxiliary note. After this the quality of tone falls off, till it becomes quite soft—according to Sherwood, *pianissimo.* From this point to the close an effective *crescendo* can be worked up to *forte* or *fortissimo.* This edition has the *mordent* on the fourth beat, instead of the third, as in other copies. The former is preferable.

In the dainty *Musette,* in G major, the thought is of peace and tranquility. The one single tone which stands out is the G in the bass. This must be pressed with sufficient weight and firmness to ensure its sounding through the four measures. As there are but sixteen measures in the whole *Musette,* this heavy G will thus be heard four times. For the rest all is smooth as oil, quite calm and neutral in tone color. It is followed by a return of the gay *Gavotte,* played through once without repeats.

The first time, however, all repeats should be observed.

MOZART 1756-1791

Mozart. This composer is perhaps best studied by the pianist through his Fantaisies. Those who are fond of teaching and playing his Sonatas exclusively may not assent to this. But with closer study they will observe that the Fantaisies are more carefully finished than the Sonatas generally are; they have more variety of theme, more subtle meaning. Many of the Sonatas were tossed off in haste, and some movements are spun out unduly.

We will now take up this "shorter" *D Minor Fantaisie,* (there is a longer one in the same key) for it is a perfect example of Mozart's most finished style. It has much variety of *tempo* and mood.

The opening *Andante* must be felt in serious mood, played with relaxed arm weight, taken slowly, even ponderously, as though forecasting some weighty matter. The *Adagio* is sweetly serene. Use the rotary, *non-legato* touch for both hands here, subduing the accompaniment and singing the melody with weight touch. When the passage in sixteenths appears, that dainty variant, which contrasts well with the more serious portions, be sure that it is played softly and phrased exactly. All depends on the proper phrasing. Of the little groups of three notes, the first is short, the second held, with down-arm weight and the third lifted off. Many students fail to understand these marks, bungle or omit them altogether, to the ruin of the passage. The last time this passage occurs it is much more difficult, and must be seriously studied to fix it securely in memory. Of course it must be studied hands separately, as every knotty passage ought to be. Recite aloud the notes of these tricky spots, thus saving time. The Cadenzas should be learned in this way. The *Allegretto* section is cheerful and childlike in its unaffected gaiety. It should be played in this spirit. Hold the *Fantaisie* in your thought in all its open-hearted sincerity, its beauty of body and spirit; so conceive and so reproduce it.

BEETHOVEN 1770-1827

When Josef Hofmann plays the first *Bagatelle,* Op. 33, we sit entranced at the exquisite art which transforms this little piece into a thing of such beauty. First there is the lovely tone, then the perfect rhythm, which preserves the balance no matter where dots, ties or rests come, or how many extra notes there are to a beat. Then the phrasing and variety of tone color. We seem to be looking at a charming landscape, full of sunshine and pleasant odors. The student often misses this beauty, from being so concerned about time and notes. For this reason it is suggested to learn each hand separately. Learn them so thoroughly that the notes can be recited. In this way the mind becomes certain of the form and meaning of the printed signs; then fingers and arms obey and are controlled by the mental powers. Let the touch be clear and pure, the phrasing well studied, accents in their places, light and shade contrasted. Note how many repetitions there are of the principal theme, also of the second theme, which enters at the first double bar. Then the extended connecting passage before the first theme reappears—those little ripples of merriment in thirty-second notes, some loud and some soft—like echoes. This passage occurs again on second page. It is well to study this *Bagatelle* with metronome, at about 60-63, to be sure that all is "in time" as well as "in tune."

MENDELSSOHN 1809-1847

It is at present the fashion in some quarters to decry Mendelssohn as old-timey and out of date; in others his music is held as about the most useful a student can take up. One learns from it how to deliver a melody with effect, while subduing the intermediate parts. His "Songs without Words" are especially admirable for this purpose; they are melodious, full of charm and delicate color. They are true songs for the piano. It is hoped the student brings to their study fingers that can deliver a melody with sympathetic touch, while holding other tones which support but do not interfere with the song.

Let us contrast two Songs widely different in style. The first is the *Barcarolle in G minor,* a Venetian boat song, in which we seem to hear the gentle lapping of the water, as we listen to the gondolier's song; or is it the song of a pair of lovers who are gliding at ease o'er the quiet sea?

In this little piece the lowest bass tones give rhythmic pulse. The melody is in the upper voice, while the accompanying notes and chords must be subdued, yet of sufficient substance to sustain and throw the melody into relief. Use arm weight to give tonal richness to the song; carefully phrase and punctuate the theme, and strive to produce tones of the necessary variety. To me this little tonal picture recalls Venice the wonderful, rising from the sea, with her marble palaces, her blue waterways and bluer skies, her picturesque bridges and towers, the graceful, dark-hued gondolas, the gay, light-hearted people. The player needs to form some such picture in mind, and allow the music to appeal to his imagination; then he may really interpret it.

Our second Song is numbered 45 and has been called a *Tarantella.* We are still under Italian skies, but the scene has shifted to Naples, where the national dance is going on. This little *Tarantella* is to be tossed off with delicate touch, with rhythmic accents, with verve and "go." A fine effect can be made with it, if the touch be clear as well as delicate and the *tempo* swift.

Among the easiest pieces of the great Pole we can select a few of the Preludes. So many immature players begin with the Nocturnes or the Valses, for which they are not prepared, when they might perform with credit a group of Preludes. Although some of these are extremely difficult, others are short and easy. Number 7, for instance, contains but two lines; it is like a tiny Mazourka, and tells its own little story.

We will first look at No. 1—likened by Huneker to a restless Impromptu. Study each hand alone. The left makes the reaches of a tenth or more, by turning the hand from side to side, using the middle key as a pivot. It will be seen that the melody is found in two voices, soprano and tenor. Practice first bringing out the upper voice; then when the piece is fully under control, study the second way, in which the thumb carries the theme. As the piece is so short, artists often repeat it, starting the repeat at the next to last measure.

Prelude No. 3 resembles a small Barcarolle, for in the left hand we have the rolling and rippling of the water and in the right a love song. Practice hands separately. The thumb in left hand must act promptly in passing under the palm, if smoothness is to be acquired. Make the right hand melody *sing,* with fingers prepared for the chords.

Prelude No. 10 has been called "Eagles' Wings,"

as those descending runs seem to beat the air. Note how simple the construction of tonic and subdominant chords. Make the runs smooth through slow practice, with firm touch; the broken chords are grasped with that sweep on the middle pivotal key and elastic closing of the fingers. A charming, flashing page of sunlight, which leads us to the portentous No. 20, in C minor.

The *Prelude in C minor* may have been the sketch for a funeral march, as someone has suggested. It expresses a dignified, noble grief. Technically and musically a tremendous effect can be made with these thirteen measures. Play throughout with legato chord movements, and relaxed arm weight. Start with full power and increase the tone at fourth measure. Look out for the E natural at fourth beat of third measure. Take pedal *after* each chord, throughout. Make the second line soft, the third yet softer, with pause on third beat of next to last measure.

LESCHETIZKY 1830-1915

The pretty piece which Leschetizky has named the *Two Larks,* has long been popular with lovers of salon music. It is melodious and well sounding, like most of the Viennese master's music. Yet in spite of its obvious charm, it is apt to be badly treated at the hands of the amateur. The melody must sing, the rhythm be correct and convincing, and the broken chord effects must ripple and glint in the sunshine like so many glistening raindrops, subdued, but clear. The piece needs a refinement of technic able to cope with the weighted melody, touch and the delicacy of the arpeggio figures. Ethel Leginska, English pianist, sometimes plays it in recital with a delicate crispness, a penetrating sweetness in the melody, that are truly delightful.

CHAPTER IV

PROGRAMME THREE

Scarlatti, *Pastorale* and *Capriccio;* Beethoven, *"Nel cor piu";* Schubert, *Impromptu F minor;* Tschaikowsky, *Troika;* Grieg, Group from Op. 43 —*Butterfly, Erotique, Little Bird;* Lavallée, *The Butterfly.*

DOMENICO SCARLATTI 1683-1757

In these Scarlatti pieces we have a couple of classic gems, which are frequently heard in the concert room and are valuable numbers for the student. Let us take an instant's glance back to the time in which they were written. The composer, Domenico Scarlatti, son of Alessandro (called the creator of modern opera), was born, it is believed, in Naples, in 1683. He studied with his father, who was really a famous composer. He himself soon learned to compose and wrote much for the harpsichord. His bold style was quite new and venturesome for those early days. He has been called the Father of modern execution; his style influenced Mendelssohn, Liszt and other moderns. He made much use of crossing hands, a novel effect at the time, and greatly developed the technique of piano playing. For the harpsichord he wrote many short pieces, most of them charming and melodious.

The two we have chosen have been edited by Tausig, who has rendered them more readable and playable for pianists of today. They are bright, cheery, even gay. We realize this old Italian master had a fund of humor, and naturally the lighthearted temperament found in southern Italy.

In the *Pastorale*—taken at whatever tempo—the curves and phrases must be delicately clear and articulate. Let the little trills contain four sixteenths to a beat. The intervals of sixths in bass, toward the close, should be fingered 4-1, 5-2, and played with rotary arm movement. The theme, after the double bar, should *sing,* with deeper tone quality, and it is recommended to make a double trill on last page, though if this is not possible it can be played in single notes. Repeat each part.

The *Capriccio* is somewhat more difficult, but requires the same delicate clearness of touch and precision of phrasing. The most refined and delicate accents and shadings are needed, also absolute evenness of touch and balance of movement and tone. When Josef Hofmann plays these pieces, as he frequently does, we wonder at the perfection of even the smallest detail; for there is perfection in touch, tone, rhythm and nuance. The student who has not this perfect sense of rhythm, should use metronome during study hours. Begin slowly, counting six, or four, as the case may be, and work up till two beats to a measure may be safely counted.

BEETHOVEN 1770-1827

Beethoven was fond of composing variations on a given theme, and, like everything he put his hand to, he ennobled this style of composition. Among the smaller sets in this form, the *"Nel cor piu"* is perhaps the finest. The theme is found as a duet in "Molinava," an old opera by Paisiello. The air is said to be long known in England as "Hope told a flattering tale." It is now destined to survive a longer time owing to Beethoven's Variations. The theme is lovely in its simple sweetness, and it must be played with purity of tone and simplicity of style.

The six Variations do not follow the plan of beginning simply and working toward the complex. They start at once with arabesques in sixteenth notes. Among these weavings of tone the melody will be found roguishly glancing out at us here and there, as though playing hide and seek. Make yourself master of the theme, and discover it, or the changes in it, in each Variation. The arabesques in the first two Variations must be delicately clear and articulate. A deeper note is sounded in Variation Four. Play a little slower, with sympathetic tone. Passage work returns in Fifth Variation, with backbone of melody in left hand. The Finale formed by the Sixth Variation is more brilliant and brings all to a fine close. Practice the piece slowly and carefully at first, to secure good tone and correct phrasing. Use metronome.

SCHUBERT 1797-1828

Schubert, like Mozart, was one of the most prolific composers who ever lived. He belongs to the
group of romantic composers, midway between Beethoven and Chopin. The lyric style of his music
often reminds one of Mendelssohn. He composed
several Sonatas, also Fantasies, Musical Moments
and Impromptus. Among eight of the last are
several favorites, though all are original and beautiful. We will select Op. 90, Number 4, in A flat
major. This Impromptu consists of a vigorous
portion, followed by a lyric middle section, after
which the first portion is exactly repeated. Put
the printed page before you and study out those
broken chords, which run through the first four
pages. You will see there are just three positions
of whatever chord is chosen, so it is easy to remember them. The little chord groups which separate
the broken chord passages may be slightly more
difficult to fix in memory, but the upper notes form
snatches of melody which can be remembered. Indeed the whole piece is filled with melody.

On the second page a bass theme starts, with
accent on second beat of each measure. Although
the passage is marked pp, it soon increases in tone,
the bass continually dominating the running figures
in right hand. On the third page a dainty lyric of
eight measures interrupts the flow of broken chord
passages; just as though the composer were so
happy he must stand still and sing out his joy.

TWO INTERESTING PIANO ALBUMS

Teachers will do well to have these albums in their libraries. The pieces in these albums may be secured separately if the teacher does not desire to place the complete album in the hands of the pupil.

SCHUBERT ALBUM

Twenty-four Compositions by Franz Schubert. Price, $1.00

If you are familiar with the beautiful melodic qualities of Schubert's compositions you will enjoy thoroughly having a volume of Schubert's numbers for piano. If you have never made the acquaintance of many of Schubert's melodies then this album holds a treat for you. The good pianist not only will find these numbers interesting, but the average player also is able to enjoy playing them, since they do not possess any forbidding keyboard work. The purchasing price is very reasonable, figuring only a little over four cents for each one of these delighting pieces.

REVERIE ALBUM

Twenty-three Melodious Pieces Price, $1.00

These numbers are of the contemplative type, and as the editors have put it in the sub-title of the book, they are "melodious and expressive pieces." Numbers such as these in the nocturne and reverie style are very acceptable for Sunday playing at home or in any religious gathering where the piano is used. They are substantial numbers that will satisfy the player and at the same time prove pleasing to hearers. We know of no more ideal collection for the average pianist who wants music to while away moments when the "day dreaming" moods prevail.

THEO. PRESSER CO.   1712-1714 Chestnut St.   **Philadelphia, Pa.**

Promptness in
Filling Orders

THIS ORDER was filled and the items sent on their way to you on the day received.

It is only one of many hundreds of all kinds similarly handled.

This happens every working day throughout the year.

No orders are held over from one day to another except those lacking in clarity or requiring special research or investigation.

Let us know if there are any unreasonable delays in the receipt of anything ordered from us or if our service disappoints you in any particular.

THEO. PRESSER CO.
1712-14 Chestnut Street, Philadelphia, Pa.

Connect those happy quarter notes, and make them join in one smooth song.

The middle section, in C sharp minor, is another song form. Play the melody with weight touch, and make it sing, to the accompaniment of the detached, light marcato chords. Correct phrasing, variety of tone, lightness and elegance are necessary to deliver this Impromptu with effect.

TSCHAIKOWSKY 1840-1893

With Tschaikowsky we enter a new tone world, where all is richly colored and pregnant with meaning. Even in his small pieces one often finds some of that intensity of feeling and expression, which, in his larger works, affect the listener so keenly.

This greatest of Russian composers has left us a number of short piano pieces, among them a set of twelve, entitled "The Seasons." The *Troika,* which we have chosen, is dedicated to November, and depicts a drive over the frozen ground in a Russian sled, drawn by three ponies. Indeed it is often called the *Three-span.* The piece is built on a brisk melody, full of vitality; it seems everything Tschaikowsky ever wrote was vital and alive. On the third line of first page, in the *arpeggio* accompaniment figures, avoid accenting thumbs. After the theme in single tones has been sung for a few lines, it is followed by the theme, now augmented to octaves and chords. At the change of key, that appoggiated chord must be snapped off in a crisp style, like the rush of a sharp wind that makes the ears tingle, and brings roses to young cheeks. The grace notes in right hand following, must be short and brittle, like points of light. Later on the first theme appears in bass, with figured accompaniment above, played staccato. Each hand must be independent here, and should be studied separately before putting together. *Troika* will be found a delightful study, full of life and "go." It seems to be a favorite of Rachmaninoff, who frequently plays it in recital.

GRIEG 1843-1907

Grieg, like Schumann and our own MacDowell, spoke in the shorter forms. His small pieces are lyric gems, crystallizing the folk songs of the people and his own emotional intensity into original and beautiful harmonies. He gathered these short pieces into groups; thus we have about twenty booklets, each containing from four to eight pieces. There are the *Poetical Tone Pictures, Op. 3;* the *Humoresque, Op. 6,* and four books of lyric *Pieces.* From the third book of these we will select three numbers, though all six can well be studied with profit.

This Norwegian composer, though he spent some years in Germany and Italy, knew Liszt and many great ones, loved his home land and lived most of

his life in Bergen, or at a neighboring country
house, where he could be surrounded by trees and
flowers. No doubt he studied bird notes at first
hand—from the feathered songsters themselves.
His *Little Bird* is a dainty bit of song, and needs
delicate handling. A soft clearness of touch for
thirty-second notes, finely marked rhythms, careful
phrasing are all necessary for its delivery. Pick
out the difficult spots, say those groups of five and
six notes on second page, and make them quite
smooth and even. Study the remainder of the little
piece with each hand alone before uniting them.
Use Metronome. When finished it must be light
and airy as a summer breeze.

The *Poéme Erotique* is in fine contrast. It is full
of intense feeling and appeal. The mood is quiet
for the first page, which contains eight measures
repeated. The phrases in both hands are very *legato*. Play the upper notes of bass chords (in first
measure the A) with octave in right. After this
passage—at the seventeenth measure, to be exact—
the unrest begins. The left hand is brought out,
then the right. After four measures, the *stretto*
begins in good earnest, and works up to a dramatic
climax, with crescendo and power, which falls off
a little, with a ritard, at the final measure before
the Tempo II. At this point the rhythm may prove
a bit troublesome, and must be quite understood
through counting and beating it out. At the third
measure the melody notes in right hand can be

joined to upper notes in bass, which will give the octaves to the right hand. This beautiful piece is a true poem in tones, finely felt and touchingly beautiful.

The familiar *Butterfly*, which can now be added to the other two is a great favorite; but often the poor little insect's wings are sadly pulled and beaten about by being subjected to heavy-handed treatment. Let us understand what is required, that this fate for the *Butterfly* may be avoided.

So many faults are apt to be passed over, that I will try to be very explicit. Even in the first measure, players will persist in putting the left hand exactly with the right on the fourth beat, when the latter should begin one note ahead. The second measure should be phrased in right hand to correspond with left. At the fourth measure from double bar, play the second half very softly, like an echo of first half.

The piece contains but sixteen measures of new matter, though there is considerable repetition. It is advised to study each hand alone, with clean touch and correct phrasing; then put them together. Gradually work up the tempo. When it can be played at the tempo the composer has indicated, you are only just ready to study it for expression and artistic effect. It should be light and delicate, with crisp accents.

Grieg sang of the mountains of his country, its trees and waterfalls, the songs and dances of the peasants, the life of the country people. His music is very subjective, always seeming to paint a picture or mood.

LAVALLEE 1842-1891

Here we have another and quite different *Butterfly*. It is perhaps the best known piece of this French-Canadian pianist, who also composed a couple of operas, an oratorio, a symphony and various smaller works.

This *Butterfly* is frankly salon music, of a brilliant and charming sort. It needs much variety of touch and tone, used in the interlocking passages, *legato, staccato leggiero*. It is an excellent study in fluency, and every player needs to cultivate this side of his equipment. If foundational principles have been thoroughly established, clearness of touch, control of fingers and arms acquired, this piece can be performed with brilliancy and effect.

CHAPTER V

PROGRAMME FOUR

Daquin, *Le Coucou;* Scarlatti, *Sonata in D major;* Mozart, *Pastorale Variée;* Schumann, *Fantaisie Stücke, Op. 12;* Raff, *La Fileuse;* Paderewski, (a) *Melodie in G flat,* (b) *Cracovienne.*

As has been our custom, we begin a new list with a taste of old-time music. For we do not wish to forget this music, which has so much of quaint charm and beauty; rather do we wish to make it live again. So we will start with a French composer who lived at the same time with Bach and Haéndel.

DAQUIN, 1693-1772

We do not forget that the clavier composers of 250 years ago had quite a different instrument from the modern piano. The sound was small and tinkling, the action light and shallow, requiring very little action or power. So the composers wrote in the style befitting their instrument; much passage work, crossing of hands, delicate runs and cadenzas, but no octaves or chords.

One of the most dainty pieces that have come down to us from long ago is the *Coucou,* by Claude

Daquin. It is so quaintly fresh that it will surely never grow old or faded. On our modern piano it sounds quite differently from what it did in the old days. It gains a richer quality of tone through the modern touch. We do not want a mere tinkling sound, we prefer a delicate, controlled *piano,* which has depth and vitality; we believe the old music gains much thereby. There are harpsichord players today who render old music on these ancient instruments. Though it is very interesting to listen to and sharpens our ears for delicate effects, I think most of us prefer our own modern piano, which is capable of such marvelous variety of color, such gradations of power and *pianissimo.* The little *Coucou* must be fine and delicate in tone, with clean touch and great attention to half lights of shading and accent. The rhythms must never be uncertain, nor the touch muddy and indistinct. It is like a piece of cobweby lace, so delicate are the arabesques. Practice at first slowly, with even, controlled finger movements.

DOMENICO SCARLATTI, 1683-1757

In the contemporary music of the Italian composer, we have the same gaiety, lightness and vivacity. Once in a while there are some tender or sad little spots, as we shall see in this Sonata, but there is always an atmosphere of style and elegance.

The Sonata chosen is a charming example of the

art of Scarlatti. It requires smooth, even technic, distinct phrasing, much light and shade. The opening figure increases in tone as it ascends to the A; its counterpart in bass does the same. Then the gay little theme enters at the third measure, while the tone grows in power to *ff* at fifth measure, where it drops at once to *piano*. These sudden changes in dynamics are characteristic of the older masters and should be observed. About the middle of first page, at the *dolce expressivo*, occurs a short passage of deeper meaning. Do not play the short note as a grace note, but a regular sixteenth—as part of the theme. A tiny child, listening to this portion of the piece, unexpectedly exclaimed—"the lady makes the piano cry!" so impressed was she by the pathos of the passage. The same passage occurs later on. The first half of the piece closes on the dominant, the second on the tonic. Analyze for chords and cadences. Work up by slow, careful study, beginning at, say 60 to a quarter note, until it will go very smoothly at more than twice that *tempo*.

MOZART, 1756-1791

We may call Mozart and Schubert the most prolific composers who ever lived, when it is remembered that each lived on this earth only about 35 years. Mozart especially left a large quantity of piano music in many forms.

One of the most delightful of Mozart's single

piano pieces is the *Pastorale Variée*. It would be interesting to know at what time of his life this graceful composition was penned—what occasion called it forth. The music suggests one of Watteau's canvases. We seem to be in the midst of a lovely French garden. There are undulating, velvety green lawns; a group of sheep in the distance; nearby merry shepherdesses and their swains are dancing. All about us are beds of gay blossoms, while fountains toss their spray high in air, till it glistens like diamonds in the sunlight.

The pretty theme, which, held to our view at different angles, like a rainbow prism—fills six lines, must be played with clearness and delicacy; the colors must be lightly laid on in pastel shades; a heavy hand will ruin their transparency. The first turn, found in 16th measure, is written out; all others are like it in that they begin on the note itself, not on the note above.

The first Variation begins on the second page, with three 16ths to a beat; later the theme is embellished with four 32nds to each count. The whole effect is *leggiero,* a delicate, ethereal lightness throughout, especially in the cadenzas of which there are two, abounding in trills and delicate tracery of passage work. The technical requirements are: a good trill, at rapid tempo, clean passage work, control of fingers, refined dynamics.

ROBERT SCHUMANN, 1810-1856

In contrast to the studies in delicacy with which our programme began, we will follow them with a couple of pieces from Schumann's *Fantaisie Stucke, Op. 12.*

Look at the *Grillen* (*Whims*). Here is plenty of good red blood, firmness, weight touch, power. The young pianist is cultivating the heavy as well as the light—force as well as delicacy—in technical work. Schumann is full of strong meat. His wonderfully rich and emotional music is often passed over by the amateur, who perhaps lacks the patience to dig for the jewels which lie just beneath the surface. *Grillen* is an excellent study in tone contrasts, rhythm and style. Fingers must be prepared and poised over the chords, to take them with precision and firmness. Hands should be practiced separately so that the phrasing shall be exact. Study pedalling carefully and do not over use it. The whole piece must glow with verve and dash.

To *Grillen* let us add the *Warum* (*Why?*) from the same set. This little piece is a general favorite, second only to the *Reverie*, from "Scenes from Childhood." It is to be played tenderly, wistfully. It asks the eternal question—Whither? Watch for the theme and do not allow accompanying voices to blot it out. Study each hand alone before playing together. At the close the question is still unanswered, and the piece dies down and fades into an inaudible murmur.

JOACHIM RAFF, 1822-1882

Raff was almost entirely self-taught in his early musical studies. At the recommendation of Mendelssohn, some of his piano pieces were published in 1843. Later he was one of the group of musicians who surrounded Liszt, and finally he became director of the Frankfort Conservatory and a teacher of composition. Edward MacDowell was his pupil, and his noble *Sonata Tragica* was inspired by his sense of loss at the death of Raff.

Perhaps Raff's greatest virtue was a gift for melody. A charming theme runs like a silver thread through the arabesques of this *Spinning Song*. The piece is a valuable addition to the repertoire of any young player, and when well played, as it used to be by William H. Sherwood, never fails to make an appeal.

Here we have true melody playing, a theme to be brought out above the subdued tracery of accompaniment. Whenever possible, it is advised to play melody in left hand over right; assisting figures are to be smooth and even. A fine study in passage playing also.

PADEREWSKI, 1860-

In remembering the marvelous pianism of the famous Pole, we are apt to forget he has written worthy music for his instrument. Among this a *Concerto, Sonata, Polish Fantaisie,* and many single pieces of charm and individuality. We select *Melodie in G flat* and the *Cracovienne*.

Those who heard him interpret these will never forget the effects produced, will never forget the searching pathos of the one or the gay abandon of the other. Let us try to reproduce in some degree, the tone quality we then heard. Young players imagine beautiful tone quality is purely a gift; they do not realize it is the fruit of many struggles and constant effort. The greatest artists have striven for it, though they were gifted to start with. In the *Melodie,* then, seek for the most singing tone possible, a clinging legato touch, and an accompaniment which supports but does not obtrude itself. A closer study of this piece shows that two parts or melodies are going at once. The second starts at 10th measure; it is the song of a man's voice, or of a 'cello. We seem to hear an impassioned girl's voice, soaring and singing, with every now and then a phrase sung by an adoring lover. Sometimes two voices blend in blissful harmony.

The *Cracovienne*—another term for *Polacca* or *Polonaise*—is a Polish Dance, filled with the gaiety and life of the people. With its incisive, infectious rhythms it sets the blood tingling and the feet dancing. It is full of color and brightness, though in the softer parts there is an undercurrent of poetic shadow, like most music of this race. The bright portions must go with great snap and brilliancy, especially the last page.

CHAPTER VI

PROGRAMME FIVE

Bach, *Two Gigues, B-flat and G major;* Beethoven, *Andante Favori;* Brahms, *Dances, Op. 39;* Grieg, *Nocturne;* Granados, *Playera;* Philipp, *Staccato Caprice.*

BACH, 1685-1750

In these little dances we have the great Bach in playful mood. They doubtless belong to his youthful period. At any rate, the gaiety and freedom of youth abound in them, especially in the second. The first, in B-flat, belongs with the *Partita, Number 1.* It seems filled with a happy content, touched with a shade of deeper feeling. The left hand contains the melody while the right hand furnishes a supporting accompaniment. Play first of all the first and fourth beats in each measure, with the left hand alone, which will give the theme; the second and third beats seem to form a secondary theme. Then play the whole left hand through, with proper touch, phrasing and arm lifting. The right hand fills in the background, with uniform phrasing throughout. The piece has an air of modernity not often found in Bach. The style is melodious and flowing. Pedaling is necessary to bring out and sustain its flowing lines.

The *Gigue (or Jig) in G major* is a madcap dance, taken from the *French Suite, No. 5*. It depends for its effect on good tone, distinct, clear touch and crisp accents. Of course it is polyphonic; Bach could scarcely write otherwise. Find as many repetitions as you can of the first subject, which occupies the first three measures. Hold all the long notes as indicated, but do not allow the sixteenths to overlap. After the double bar the theme enters on the dominant. Later, as in the first half, it is broken up into parts, woven in and out in a fascinating way. Work up with metronome, starting at about 72 to a quarter note, until it can be played to more than double the speed, counting but two in a measure.

BEETHOVEN, 1770-1827

Beethoven's famous *Andante Favori* is one of those pieces that give a feeling of complete satisfaction and content. It has much variety in passage work and technical forms, but they are merely woven in and around one of the loveliest themes the master ever penned. Here are atmosphere, tonal balance, the melodic line—indeed everything to be thought of. The theme must above all *sing*, with tenderness and sweetness, over the tones that accompany it. The delicate passage work if often staccato and must be smooth and even. The passage in thirds can be played by fingers 2-4, and is then much easier and surer. The Variations increase in difficulty toward the close. If the octaves prove a stumbling block, make a special study of them, hands singly and together, also octave scales in this key. The short coda recites the theme again, like a farewell, in which good-byes are reiterated several times.

BRAHMS, 1833-1897

Brahms, whose music we take up for the first time in this program, was one of the immortal composers whose compositions are becoming more known and loved as time passes. His piano music is among the most distinctive and original we have. It is strong, virile, rugged, sometimes even harsh; but there is always a glint of tenderness and sweetness just back of the harshness, as the sun shines behind a cloud.

Among the most charming things Brahms composed for the piano, are the *Valses, Op. 39*. There are sixteen in the set, each more beautiful than the last, if that could be. Pianists are beginning to pay more attention to this lovely group of tonal and rhythmic fancies.

The young pianist can gather a group of the Valses, like a nosegay of fragrant flowers. Include in it Numbers 1, 2, 3, 4, 8, 9, 10, and above all 15. No. 1 is stirring and brilliant, with its octave skips;

there is a lot of "go" in the single page. No. 2 is
sweet and alluring, a spiritualized dance; while No.
3 is in the same mood. No. 4 is virile and passionate; vigor throbs in every phrase. No. 8 is full of
persuasive entreaty, and needs smoothness and
lovely tone. No. 9 is even more tender and expressive. No. 10 is in a jesting vein; its double
third scales must be even and smooth, with little
upward crescendos. No. 15 is perhaps the best
known of them all. In moderate tempo, the tender
theme is sweet and soothing. A part of the second
half is often repeated, thus lengthening the little
piece, which is all too short. The triplets near the
end must be smoothly legato and subdued. The
selection we have suggested will give a good idea
of the whole set, but doubtless the earnest student
will desire to know them all. These *Dances* are
transcribed for four hands and also for piano and
violin. We shall later take up other compositions
of Brahms; in this program we meet him on his
most ingratiating and lovable side.

GRIEG, 1843-1907

We have already used some of the shorter pieces
of this composer, and have thus become somewhat
familiar with his unique style, which is really unlike that of any other composer.

We will now take up his *Nocturne,* probably the
only one he ever wrote. It is found in the fifth

volume of the "Lyrical Pieces, Op. 54," among such companions as *March of the Dwarfs, Shepherd Boy, Scherzo,* and others. The *Nocturne* is a beautifully polished gem, a perfect example of Grieg's individual art. Beginning softly, with few words (notes), the chief theme is found in right hand with the rhythm of two notes against three in the accompaniment. At top of second page a new passage enters, like the fluttering and trilling of little birds. How often Grieg introduces bird voices into his music.

Now comes the *Piu Mosso.* This starts *una corda,* with soft pedal—and, like the growing of some deep, inward passion, rises to a big climax at the double *forte;* then it dies down like a sobbing child hushed into silence. The first part now returns, a little more enlarged this time. Note the beautiful shifting harmonies on the last page, first six measures. Watch the pedalling that the harmonies are kept clear and are not blurred. This passage is followed by a few more bird-like trills and the piece closes with a couple of long-drawn chords, which ought to have something of the sustained character of strings; indeed the piece lends itself well to violin transcription.

ENRIQUE GRANADOS

When this Spanish composer came to America a few years ago, to witness the premiere of his opera "Goyescas," his music was almost unknown here.   We realize Spanish composers are not greatly inclined to write for our instrument, more's the pity; for the music of Spain reflects the fascinating rhythms, the gaiety and color, the langorous enticement of that land of dreams and castles.

With the coming of Granados, we learned to know his opera and some of his piano music, part of it based on themes found in the opera. A couple of these pieces Ernest Schelling, a warm friend of the composer, had already brought out. Now the composer played them himself, and we found he was an excellent pianist. The few recitals of his own music which he gave during his brief stay in America were unique events. Those who attended appreciated the rare treat; they could not guess the gifted composer would be lost during the voyage home, on the ill-fated ship, sent to the bottom by an enemy bomb.

Among the few piano pieces Granados has left us are a brilliant Polonaise-like piece called *El Pelele*, and a Spanish dance termed *Playera;* the latter on our present program.

The *Playera, Op. 5, No. 5*, has all the Spanish characteristics just mentioned; it is gay and bright, yet there is ever an undercurrent of brooding, a grey thread among the gold, a smile and a tear together. The droning bass forms a continuous background, like the strumming of a guitar, which it probably represents. The left hand, especially in measures where grace notes occur, should indicate the plucking of strings, sometimes subdued, again accented, as indicated. The rhythmic swing should always be preserved; rhythm is the very heartbeat and life of music; without rhythm we should not have music. At the *Andante* the theme must sing with increased beauty of tone and fervency of expression; with clinging legato and sufficient pedal to color and sustain the theme without blurring the harmonies. After this melodious middle section, the Dance proper is identically repeated, closing as it began, in E minor, and with a long retard. Guiomar Novaes uses this Dance on her programmes with the happiest effect.

ISIDOR PHILIPP, 1863-

This Hungarian-French composer has been a Professor of piano at the Paris Conservatoire ever since 1893. He is an excellent pianist, a teacher of exceptional gifts and has composed some brilliant solos and popular Studies.

Perhaps his best-known composition for piano is the *Staccato Caprice,* with which we close our programme. It is dashing and effective. Those interlocking sixths prove most useful practice. Prepare for the attack by poising the hand above the keys with fingers correctly spaced to fit the intervals. Practice slowly, with firm fingers and with flexible wrists and arms. When technically correct, gradually increase the tempo, till there is sufficient fluency to add expression marks and pedalling.

CHAPTER VII

PROGRAMME SIX

Mozart, *Sonata in A major;* Schubert, *Moment Musical, No. 6; Impromptu in B flat major, Op. 142;* Chopin, *Nocturne in F minor; Mazurka in A flat major, Op. 50, No. 2; Valse in F major;* Liszt, *Mazurka.*

The serious piano student finds himself advancing by rapid strides from the simple programmes with which we began to the one taken up in this chapter. Such progress cannot be accomplished in a few months. He may feel well content if after a couple of years he can measure up to the compositions suggested. He cannot hope to do so unless he is at the same time keeping hard at work at the technical forms so carefully laid down in "Self Help in Piano Study," or in other technical material of like nature. Only by persistent effort, guided by carefully controlled intelligence will technical facility keep pace with the desire to play pieces fluently and effectively.

MOZART, 1756-1791

We begin our recital with a work by Mozart, the ever youthful, beautiful, immortal master. We have already studied some of his shorter pieces; now we shall undertake one of the finest Sonatas in the whole list of eighteen.

The Sonata Form is the highest in instrumental music. It consists generally of three parts or movements of contrasted material and meaning. The first movement is usually of a lively, vigorous character, with several contrasted themes, developed according to special rules. The second movement is shorter, slower, containing a serious theme or song-like melody. The third is often in rondo form, which means the germ theme, or motto, keeps ever returning, like a "round."

Sonatas may have more or fewer than three parts. The Sonata Form has been a favorite with the greatest masters, from Mozart and Haydn down. Beethoven wrote thirty-eight; Schubert, Schumann, Chopin, Brahms several each; even Liszt wrote one of unique character.

The Sonata Form is the form of the Symphony, String Quartet, Piano Trio, Quartet or Quintet. The learner will find the subject a most interesting one for further study; we counsel him to analyze each movement into motive, section, phrase and period.

The Sonata here chosen is not one of the easy ones, nor is it in quite the regular form. Its first movement consists of an Air with Variations, while instead of a slow middle movement, there is a

Menuette. The third part is in regular Rondo form.

First of all study and memorize the theme. Note how simple its construction and chord progressions; how regular its form and how beautiful the effects obtained. Each half of the theme has eight measures, with a cunning little coda of two measures added at end of second half. Observe all accent, touch and phrasing signs. Some artists play the theme semi-staccato throughout, but it seems more logical to use legato touch with careful phrasing.

Variation 1. Phrase carefully, with combined movements in right hand and with light staccato in left. Contrast the light and shade, the brightness and the shadow, as directed in the music. The melody lies hidden behind the notes in this first Variation. In Variation 2 it is frankly in the right hand and always prominent. The grace notes in bass must be crisp and sharp, in order to gain color and variety. The 3rd Variation, in minor, must be smoothly legato, with constantly shifting light and shade. Variation 4, in happier mood, is smooth, flowing and genial. In the 5th Variation we really have a slow movement, with numerous ornaments and embellishments, all of which must be in perfect rhythm, and given with tonal variety. Variation 6 is gay and bright, and in rapid tempo.

In place of the usual slow movement we have a spirited Menuette, with plenty of light and shade. The final movement is the famous Turkish Rondo, a charming number, which can be used separately. Do not make the mistake of taking this movement too fast. It is marked Allegretto, not Allegro or Presto. Even though the greatest pianists elect to play it with great rapidity, our sense of fitness and beauty does not approve. Be sure to use repeats all through, with both endings to each Variation.

FRANZ SCHUBERT, 1791-1828

Franz Schubert was, like Mozart, a born melodist; in his short life of thirty-one years, he accomplished marvels by his creative genius. He wrote in all forms with consummate mastery. Liszt called Schubert "the most poetic musician who ever lived." His music always makes a touching appeal, perhaps because he knew poverty and sorrow, and never attained worldly success. Yet he was one of the wealthiest of men, since he possessed a rich fund of melody and harmony, and an inexhaustible flow of musical ideas.

Among Schubert's piano pieces are two groups of Impromptus and one group of *Moments Musicals*. We will select one from the last and pair it with one of the Impromptus.

Six pieces fill the group of *Moments Musicals, Op. 94*. They were published in 1828, the year he passed away, and have been called his greatest achievement for the piano. Each one is a gem; the 6th has been thus poetically described: "This is perhaps Schubert's most profound piano piece. A revery in still chords, which lulls us with its pensive and delicate sorrow, its singing imitations, its magic enharmonics, its sweet melodies rising like flowers from the soft ground." It is indeed a study in legato chords, and requires arm weight and control. Strive to bring out and accentuate the top note of the chords which carries the melody.

We will follow this moon-lighted revery by the familiar *Impromptu in B flat*. This piece should be in the repertoire of every pianist and teacher. Huneker wrote of it: "How melodious is the theme, how the spirit mounts with each variation, so dramatic in the minor; the picture at the close dissolves in foaming scales!"

Analyze the theme for key and chord progressions. The form is quite regular; four-measure lines, with the little two-measure conclusions at the end. In Variation 1, be sure to connect the melody notes in the upper voice; consider they form a line of silver song above a spray of accompanying sound. Subdue this accompaniment, especially when played by first and second fingers. Play Variations 2 in bright, snappy fashion; the second half of it begins with heavy arm weight, but finishes delicately in those descending staccato scales. Variation 3; use relaxed arm weight in this dramatic variation. After the double bar heavy weight should be again used; the *pp* passage should be soft, velvety and *legato*.

Variation 4 has the melody a part of the time in the bass; this must be brought out. In Variation 5 we have the "foaming scales," which must be very smooth and even. The impressive *Coda* of eight measures brings this lovely work to a fitting conclusion. It is often called the "Rosamunde Impromptu," as the same theme occurs in the "Rosamunde" music.

CHOPIN, 1810-1849

Of Chopin, piano poet, we choose a short group, including several styles.

The *F major Nocturne, Op. 15, No. 1,* is all too infrequently played, yet it is both sweetly lyric and dramatic. Make the right hand theme sing, with melody touch and relaxed arm weight, above the rocking accompaniment in the left hand. In the middle section, the left hand thunders up and down several times. This passage, by way of contrast to what has gone before, must be strongly brought out. Between these passages and the return of the first song lies a haunting phrase for the soprano which should be pressed out. The return of the first portion is effected softly; from here on to the end the whole section can be subdued, as if in shadow.

As a contrast to this Nocturne, the *F minor Etude* may be attempted. This composition cannot be mastered in a week or a month. But the sooner it is begun the sooner is there a chance for it to grow into the fingers. It is indeed a growth, if started—like a tiny seedling—with slow, careful finger action and evenness of tone and movement. Each day, each week, it will gain in smoothness, control and velocity. Part of the time it can be played with metronome and on the practice clavier (if possible). Much slow practice will keep it smooth. Learn the hands separately before attempting to put them together, and be sure to preserve correct rhythms.

The *Mazourka in A flat* is charming as well as aristocratic. The present writer heard this piece years ago, played by Mme. Essipoff, and its grace and charm made a deep and lasting impression. The style of this Mazourka is elegant and distinguished —just as one would imagine Chopin would write— or play. While the notes are not of themselves difficult, it is not so easy to play this piece with the needed finesse and nuance. The right hand should be prominent throughout. The D flat Trio, with the episode in relative minor, are graceful and should be deftly managed. This is the first Mazourka we have attempted, and one needs to get into the spirit of these rhythms. Chopin wrote fifty-two of these Polish dances; they form a veritable treasure trove of beauty and charm.

To conclude the group, play *Valse in F major*. The opening chords should be well rolled and crescendo. The arabesques begin to spin softly at first, then increase in tone. For two pages they weave a dainty web, which must be quite under control before the necessary tone shadings can be effected. On the third page the grace notes begin; they must be crisp and exact; also the trills should generally have four sixteenths to a beat. At the fourth page the first passage returns; the short *Coda* is brilliant and is to be played fortissimo.

FRANZ LISZT, 1810-1886

It will now be interesting to study a *Mazurka* of Liszt, the only one he ever wrote. A brilliant introduction of eight measures leads to the entrance of the first theme in double notes. The piece is very rhythmic, with marked accents, plenty of dash and style. An elegant salon piece, such as Liszt himself might dash off, when he deigned to gratify his admirers at a soirée. It requires good technical command in staccato sixths and octaves, resonant chords, rhythmic left hand and clean phrasing. Through careful study of such a composition, the pianist acquires style and elegance; provided the technique is adequate and the many marks of phrasing, expression and dynamics are carefully observed.

CHAPTER VIII

PROGRAMME SEVEN

Mendelssohn, *Etude in B flat minor;* Beethoven, *Menuet, E flat, Ecossaise;* Grieg, *Sonata, Op. 7;* Brahms, *Intermezzo, E major; Capriccio, B minor;* Rubinstein, *Barcarolle, G major,* and *Valse Allemagne.*

MENDELSSOHN, 1809-1847

James Huneker once remarked of Mendelssohn's music, that his compositions are individual, perfect in structure, piquant and pianistic. "Are not the smaller pieces, the Caprices, Scherzos and Fantaisies, worthy the virtuoso?" he asked. "They are more difficult than they seem, demanding impeccable finger technic, a feathery wrist and incisive accentuations." These are just the qualities required of the player, especially the clean-cut, immaculate articulation and the delicate accents; he will do well to bear these salient points in mind, and bind them on his forehead, when he attempts the music of this composer.

The *Etude in B flat minor* is a gem among Mendelssohn's shorter pieces. It is a study in melody playing, for it is built of a flowing theme, supported

by a background of lace-like arpeggios. To the
lover of Mendelssohn's music—and who can help
loving it?—the melody which sings through the
piece is one of the most inspired of his creations. It
must be the first thing in the piece that is studied,
and should be clearly in mind before anything else
is attempted.

Play the melody through alone, striving to produce a beautiful tone with correct phrasing. Then
strive to realize something of the inner meaning of
this theme, the spiritual meaning and significance
of the long, smooth phrases. Only so can we begin to apprehend, feel and bring out the message
the composer seeks to convey. As the melody alternates between the two hands, it should be so connected that we cannot discover which hand is playing it, since both should be equally smooth and even.

The arpeggio accompaniment moves up and
down, or rather backward and forward, smoothly
and evenly. It is to be practiced slowly at first, and
seeing that the backward movement is considerably
more difficult than the forward, great care should
be taken to pass the thumb quickly under the hand,
avoiding all jerk. The hand, as is well known,
should be slanted obliquely across the keys. Play
the trill, which occurs in the left hand twice, in
thirty-second notes, two to each sixteenth in the
arpeggio figure. On the last page, play the theme
in octaves, with arm-weighted touch. Make every
phrase tell in this nobly beautiful piece, and finally

weld all into one harmonious, expressive, dignified whole.

BEETHOVEN, 1770-1827

From Beethoven, who, as we know, joined the classic perfection of form to the more romantic freedom of manner, thus forming the great link between the classic and modern music, we will choose two unique yet short pieces, a *Menuet* and an *Ecossaise*.

The *Menuet in E flat*—not to be confounded with the familiar one belonging to the *E flat Sonata, Op. 31, No. 3*—stands quite alone, and its spirit seems to be one of a calm content. It appears to be one of those fugitive expressions of the master, caught when he was evidently in a happy frame of mind. No one had irritated or opposed; the world, for the moment, looked bright; the sun shone and skies were blue. Perhaps he had had a refreshing ramble in wood or field, and expressed his satisfaction in this charming little piece. First analyze it for phrases and periods. Play the double thirds in the first measure with pure legato touch, the chords in third and fourth, and seventh and eight measures, with lifted arm. Always bring out the voices which carry the theme. The *Trio* should be smooth and flowing, with phrases separated by lifted arm and hand. The four measures of octaves are more vigorous, and have decisive rhythmic accents. Close with a return to the *Menuet*, played without repeats.

The *Ecossaises* seem to have been lately discovered. They come to us edited and prepared for concert performance by Busoni. One wonders where these Scottish dances have been hiding for so many years; however we have them now and they are a charming addition to the pianist's repertoire.

The Dances are five in number, each new one being separated from the others by a repetition of the first Dance, used as a sort of a refrain. The aim of the player should be, first to secure clearness of form and phrasing, then variety of touch and tone; otherwise the frequent repetition of the refrain tends to monotony. Variety in touch, tone and expression, is essential!

GRIEG, 1843-1907

It is said that Grieg in his music, did what Gade seemed to shrink from; that is he employed racial characteristics, and Scandinavian idioms, giving through these a unique charm to his compositions. We have in former programmes, used some of the shorter pieces, which are little gems in their way. Yet the composer shows he could work in the larger forms, for there are the two fine sonatas for violin and piano, the 'cello sonata, and the sonata for piano, Op. 7.

Among the longer works for piano, this *Sonata in E minor* stands out as representative of the larger

Grieg.   It is worthy to be placed with the *Ballade* and the *Holberg Suite*.   The Sonata is full of fresh beauty and perennial charm, and should be familiar to every serious student of the instrument.

The work contains four contrasted movements. Let us study them together.

The opening theme reveals a quiet nobility of mood.   Beginning softly, it increases in tone till the passage ends in a burst of power expressed in several strong, elastic chords.   The theme now starts again, this time in octaves, with accents and full power.   An elaboration of the theme continues the stress, until a few soft chords lead to the second theme.   Let the chords and octaves of this first page be crisp and firm, with arm weight combined with elastic fingers and rhythmic accents.

The second theme starts on last line of first page. It stands well out in bass, while the right hand accompanies with little figures in sixteenth notes.   At first the mood is quiet, but restlessness soon sets in and we have a climax at top of second page.   A third theme now enters, a characteristic, freakish little tune, like a tiny jest between more serious thoughts.   At the *a tempo,* a flowing melody appears, a lovely song, though "short breathed,"—as Grieg so often is.

The first theme, now in the major, enters for the third time.   It is again *fortissimo* and leads to the passage in 6/8 rhythm and change of key, a kind of dialogue between soprano and bass.   This continues for the space of a page, until the first theme reappears. From here on to the end of the movement, the various themes already brought forward are heard again, and the movement closes with a fine climax of power.

The *Andante,* in C major, opens with a sonorous and expressive theme, first in single notes and later in octaves. The theme seems to be declaimed in two portions, both of which occupy the first page. Now intervenes a playful little passage, culminating in a big crescendo, and leading to the first theme, announced with splendid sonorous chords, over arpeggio figures in the left hand, and worked up to a strong climax. The second part of the theme, with its modifications, fills the last page, and the movement ends quietly, slowly and softly, with a prolonged tonic chord.

In the *Menuette* we have a short piece full of vigor and life. Its incisive rhythmic swing must be felt and brought out by the player. There are strong contrasts of light and shade, now delicate and insinuating, now vigorous to the verge of boisterousness. Those Norwegian peasants, with the rhythm of the race in their veins, are enjoying themselves on one of their fete days, and Grieg has embodied the vigorous life of it in his *Menuette.* There are some irregular rhythms too, which must be equalized and brought into harmony with the rest.

A wholly delightful movement is the *Finale,* light,

delicate, swift, with shifting themes, short but sweet, a dainty nosegay of melodies. After a rising crescendo, a powerful and grandiose passage occurs on the last page, like a pæon of victory.

The pianist requires a clean, sure technic, arm-weight power for chords and octaves, and the ability to express the varying moods as they follow each other in constantly changing succession.

BRAHMS, 1833-1897

Von Bülow classed Brahms with Bach and Beethoven, as one of the "Three B's." The world has not yet fathomed the greatness of Brahms. There is a large amount of wonderful music yet to be explored. Brahms was both a philosopher and a poet; his music does not appeal to the superficial, to those who do not think. The thoughtful, earnest student and player will find in this composer's piano music a wealth of meaning which will be a constant source of surprise and delight.

Let us choose two contrasting numbers, each a gem in its own way. The *Intermezzo in E major* is one of the seven pieces brought out as Op. 116, under the general title of *Fantaisies*. It is a suave, quiet melody, found in the upper voice of continuous chord progressions. The performer must bring out this theme by making the finger playing the top note of the chords a little firmer and more extended —*longer*—than the others. Brahms is noted for his irregular rhythms, and in this *Intermezzo* he makes much use of triplets against two notes. The idea seems to be expressed in short sections of two measures each, and the player should pause slightly—take breath as it were—between these phrases. Indeed there are many pauses, rhetorical and other, which should be observed. The first and third pages are in the same vein, separated by a middle section containing another melody, but the same rhythmical problems of two notes against three. This page, in its calm, serene beauty, reminds one of Mendelssohn.

We will follow this lyric tone poem with the delightful *Capriccio in B minor, Op. 76.* This is a real caprice, bright, gay, even jocose. Here is a chance to practice crisp staccatos, accents, exact phrasing, tone color and atmosphere. The third page contains an expressive melody, and is taken at a slightly slower tempo. At the same time the accompaniment is staccato. On the fifth page the first theme is combined with other notes which should not hide or overshadow it. The *B minor Capriccio* is a test of the player's accuracy, in technical equipment and performance; but beyond these, of his esprit and ability to make such a piece sparkle and glow with life.

ANTON RUBINSTEIN, 1830-1894

Rubinstein was one of the greatest pianists of his time, a man of exquisite sense for tone color; his playing combined tremendous power with the finest delicacy. When he thundered the *Turkish March,* from Beethoven's "Ruins of Athens," we held our breath, startled with such overwhelming force. The piano was a full orchestra; that was the effect he wanted. Then he played Chopin's *Berceuse* with those velvet fingers, it was as the night breeze sighing over perfumed flowers. No other pianist had such command of tonal gradations; it was marvelous, and remains a fragrant memory.

A pianist and composer of such skill ought to write effectively for his instrument. Among his admired solos are the *Barcarolles,* a set of five sea pieces. The *G major Barcarolle* is one of the most perfect of these. It is a study in double thirds. The pianist who would master it is advised to practice double third scales in all keys, using the C fingering. For the first page of the piece the floating figures of double thirds wave up and down without saying anything definite; they merely create atmosphere. The song itself begins on the second page; the accompanying chords are to be subdued and liquid. When the double third figures reappear, a penetrating melody in the bass is added; this must dominate the passage. The piece is full of atmosphere and must be played in smooth, flowing style.

The *Valse Allemagne* is found in the set of *Popular Dances, Op. 82.* Though not so difficult as the well-known *Valse Caprice,* it is brilliant and effective. Take the piece in detail for clean finger action, correct phrasing, accent and decisive rhythm. Study variety of tone color and dynamics, with careful pedalling. The piece can be made very striking and effective.

CHAPTER IX

PROGRAMME EIGHT

Rameau, *Theme and Variations in A minor;* Beethoven *Contra Dances, Numbers 1, 2, 3;* Schumann, *Arabesque, Nachtstück, No. 4, Novellette in E major;* Eric Korngold, Three Numbers from *Fairy Suite;* Cyril Scott, *Danse Negre;* Moszkowski, *Ungeduld.*

RAMEAU, 1683-1764

Jean Philippe Rameau was one of the early French composers, and was contemporary with Bach and Handel, being born two years before them. He was a conspicuous figure in his time and did much to advance the art of music in various directions. He even concerned himself with improving the theory of music and published a "New System of Musical Theory." He was the author of a number of operas, songs and clavichord pieces. A few of these last have been edited and adapted to our instrument; no doubt there are many more waiting to be discovered.

There is a freshness and grace about this early music, which is captivating. Even when the minor mode is used, the ideas are generally bright and gay, with a certain lightheartedness and elegance.

The *Theme and Variations* is about the most ambitious piano piece of Rameau with which we are familiar. The *Theme* itself is well planned, dignified and expressive. In some editions of the piece, the theme is overlaid with turns and ornaments, quite in the manner of writing for the voice in those days, by Italian composers. When Mme. Annette Essipoff played it on her American tour, years ago, she gave out the theme quite simply, leaving off most of the ornaments. An edition of the piece, issued at that time, gave the music as she played it; the edition may, however, be now out of print.

The theme is to be announced in a clear, straightforward manner, with simple elegance. A mordent may be used to begin the second measure, also a mordent on the second beat of the fifth measure, and a short trill on the second beat of the third measure. At second half of theme, a mordent on the first beat of 2nd, 4th and 6th measures and a turn on the second beat of the 7th measure will give sufficient ornamentation.

Variation 1 has the theme in the left hand, overlaid with delicate arabesques in the right. These must be smooth and flowing. In the one octave scales which make up the second half of the Variation, variety may be secured through dynamic treatment of these scales, making some louder while others are softer.

The 2nd Variation follows the opposite course, having scales in the left hand and melody chords in the right. The upper note of these chords carries the theme and should stand out above the other tones of the chord. Variation 3 is more difficult, in that it carries in the right hand the melody interwoven with the accompaniment.

The 4th Variation requires crisp, exact staccato touch, with well-defined accents. The 5th and 6th Variations form a pair, counterparts of the same device of contracting and extending the hand and changing fingers on the same key. At the close a fine effect is made with an extended trill on the G-sharp before the final chord.

This beautiful example of old-time music is not as easy as it seems at first glance, and should be attempted only by the player with well-developed finger action and control of his playing mechanism. If he can add to these a comprehension of the lightness and elegance with which such music is to be played, the rhythmic precision and delicacy of shading required, he will play it with success.

BEETHOVEN, 1770-1827

The Country Dances, or Contra Tänze, to use the original title, are delightful bits of humor to teach and to play. They are very rhythmic, full of life, and give us a glimpse of the master from another angle. Beethoven, during his frequent wanderings about the countryside, had doubtless many times met with peasants or country folk enjoying their merry-making on the green. At all events he has caught the spirit of country life with its carefree gaiety, and has embodied it in these unusual dances.

Number one is perhaps the most finished of the three. An *Allegro Moderato* movement of four pages in length, it starts off brightly in the key of C, with staccato left hand and themes in the right. Attention to variety of touch and phrasing will make the picture alive. The middle section, in G, is more lyric in vein, while the piece closes with a repetition of the first part.

Each dance is complete in itself and can be used separately. Each has a contrasted middle portion, ending with a return of the first section. The first and third dances are in C major; No. two is in E-flat, with the middle portion in A-flat. When played with understanding and variety of touch and tone, these dances give brightness and humor to a programme.

ROBERT SCHUMANN, 1810-1856

We have followed this favorite composer from his earliest little pieces, taken from the "Album for the Young," to the *Fantaisie Pieces, Op. 12,* and now to the *Arabesque, Op. 18.* This piece, as well as the other two chosen for the present programme, belongs to those wonderful romantic years when

Schumann wrote exclusively for the piano. In a letter to Clara Wieck, he mentions composing the *Arabesque,* "which is not on any theme, and in which everything is curiously interwoven." He directs the principal movement to be played "lightly and delicately." The *Arabesque* is, nevertheless, full of melody, in spite of Schumann's remark about it. The first two pages contain this melodic tracery in the upper voice, which, like the first Variation of Schubert's *Rosamund Impromptu,* which we lately studied, must be played legato, and be heard above the accompaniment.

The second section, a Variant in E minor, is sturdy and insistent; the figure is repeated over and over, rising from *mf* to *f* and finally to *ff* in the last line. From here a lovely, dreamy passage of about sixteen measures connects with the first portion of the piece, which is an exact repetition of the first two pages. This is followed by a second Variant, in A minor, conceived in true argumentative style; the composer is having a humorous dispute with someone, and he seems to be getting the best of it. The first movement now returns for the second time.

The *Coda,* of sixteen measures, is reflective and dreamily poetic; indeed the whole piece gives a glimpse—a vision of the inner world of the composer.

The *Night Pieces, Op. 23,* are four in number, though the last one is usually chosen for concert use. And that one is so lovely that it is no wonder its beauty has overshadowed that of the others. Note the mysterious harmonies which occur in the two opening measures. They usher us into the sweet, cool, night consciousness, where all is peaceful and serene. The melody is found in the upper note of the right hand chords, which must be quickly rolled, putting the left hand octaves with the first note of chord, and holding the melody note as long as possible to sustain it. It is necessary to turn the hand from side to side, to accomplish this effect. Practice the chords alone using the middle key as a pivot, and learning to swing the hand from side to side, with loose arm. At the change of key, on second page, bring out the figures which alternate between the hands. Take the last line still slower; the two groups of six sixteenths are more effective if played somewhat stronger, thus standing out as a slightly discordant suggestion, which is soon hushed in the calm peace of the close. This piece should not be played faster than a quarter note to 60, though often marked 96.

The eight stirring compositions called *Novellettes, Op. 21,* are not all familiar to students. They are each and all of great interest, full of intellectual meat, poetic or stirring, as the case may be.

Let us look closely at No. 7, in E major. It opens with vigorous octaves, which reach a climax on the A, in fourth measure, and again at the heavy chord at fifteenth measure, after the long octave passage. These octaves must be played with free, loose arm, also with loose wrist, and with controlled power and weight. Now follows a charming passage in which the same theme appears in single notes, the short phrases being tossed back from•one hand to the other, and in the key of C; the octaves reappearing at the close. Next comes an intervening passage of thirds, which must be well phrased to bring out its meaning. This is followed by the octave passage in the original key.

The middle portion of the *Novellette* consists of a lyric section, a lovely song in upper voice, supported by an undulating accompaniment. This melody, which somehow reminds one of Chopin, must be played legato, with arm weight; it requires beautiful tone and poetic treatment. After it the first and third themes fill the remaining page.

ERIC KORNGOLD, 1897-

Let us now leap from the romantic Schumann of a former decade, to one of the romantic moderns; from the music of three quarters of a century ago to the music of today. We will choose some examples from a unique and precocious modern composer, young Eric Korngold, who was born at Brünn, May 29, 1897, and began to play and write music about as soon as he could speak. The set of seven piano pieces, Op. 3, which he calls *Fairy Pictures,* were composed in 1910, when the

boy was thirteen. He has named them *The En-
chanted Princess, Rubezahl, The Brownies, The
Fairy King's Ball, The Brave Little Tailor,* and
Epilogue. Young teachers and players are advised
to become familiar with these unique pieces, for
Korngold is a coming composer to be reckoned
with. The idiom will sound strange to your ears
at first, but keep on tasting; you will soon like the
tang, and will learn to enjoy the quaint melodies
and unusual harmonies. Each piece tells a story.
Take *The Real Princess,* its ascending theme fairly
talks. In playing you will find it all weight touch,
rich tone quality, accents, crescendos, and dramatic
climaxes. The coda is to be very subdued, and is
made more impressive by the preceding fortissimo
passage.

The *Real Princess* may be followed by the fifth
of the set, *The Fairy King's Ball,* also a vivid picture in tones. First there is a blare of trumpets
summoning the guests to the royal festivities; next
a merry Valse peeps out here and there. But there
are other entertainments and diversions besides
dancing, for there are dramatic episodes, gay bustle
and the confusion of chatter, just as there would
naturally be at such a function; for the guests are
having a delightful time of it. The player needs
good technic, ability to paint in strong colors, and
a lively imagination to picture to himself what it all
means, and to reproduce the picture effectively.

The *Epilogue* is a charming bit, which weaves

into its mesh some of the themes from the princess.
We seem to be waving her a tender farewell.

CYRIL SCOTT, 1879-

One of the newer men of England is Cyril Scott.
Of him Debussy wrote: "Cyril Scott is one of the
rarest artists of the present generation. His piano
works merit recognition from all who are in any
way interested in the trend of modern music."

As no wide-awake teacher or player can afford
to ignore the trend of modern music, let us by all
means study the compositions of this new master,
who has written so ingratiatingly for our instrument. Though we add but one of his pieces to this
programme, the player can include the *Lotus Land,
Sea Marge,* and *Valse Caprice* also.

The *Danse Negre* is a fascinating bit of local
color, requiring clean touch combined with velocity
and a command of light and shade. The last page
is the most difficult, as the harmony shifts at every
beat. For the *glissando* run it is recommended to
use third finger, with the hand slanted outward
(just the opposite from the regular scale relation
of hand to the keys). *Glissando,* however, is a
somewhat individual matter, and some players may
find the use of another finger more convenient.

MOSZKOWSKI, 1854-

Moritz Moszkowski, a native of Breslau, has resided in Paris for a quarter of a century. He has composed charming piano music in the lighter style, and has been one of the famous artist-teachers to whom many Americans have gone for finish and prestige. He was also reckoned as one of the famous pianists of the day. He understands the resources of the instrument and has put out many brilliant bravoura compositions.

A set of five salon pieces under the title of "Spring," contains the short, effective number called *Impatience*. It is the first of the set, and is a splendid technical study as well as a bit of brilliant bravoura. Octaves in right hand form the theme throughout, combined with groups of thirds and fourths. The bass supports and gives rhythmic emphasis to what the other hand is doing. The impression is of vivid life, of constant movement, as though a spirited pony were racing over the plain. This feeling of rushing movement takes possession of the player, impelling him to play the piece over and over, just for the exhilaration of the doing. Bring out the theme in octaves, subduing the accompanying notes, but do not stiffen the wrist, as there is a temptation to do. Work up a brilliant crescendo at the close. A sprightly and valuable number.

CHAPTER X

PROGRAMME NINE

D'Albert, Part of *Suite, Op. 1;* Schumann, *Kreisleriana, Nos. 1, 4, 5, 6, 8;* Scriabine, *Nocturne for Left Hand Alone;* Rachmaninoff, *Prelude in G minor;* Chopin-Liszt, *Maiden's Wish;* Liszt, *Rhapsodie Number 4.*

Eugen d'Albert is one of the piano giants of our time. He has lived so long in Germany and is so associated with its musical life that one is apt to forget or to overlook the fact that he was born in Glasgow, Scotland, and that his early musical education was pursued in London, under Pauer, Prout, Stainer and Sullivan. Later, after years of study in Vienna and association with Liszt, he burst upon the world, a great artist of the keyboard. What technic, what power, velocity, velvety softness combined with breadth and nobility of tone and style! Recital after recital was given in Berlin and other cities, at the outset of his career. On a certain well-remembered occasion he played a programme lasting two hours, one afternoon, at Carl Klindworth's, for the American pupils. He was in glorious mood that day and gave an unforgettable performance.

D'Albert has written a number of operas, two piano concertos, and some piano solos. In the

Suite Op. 1, we have an imitation of the old style of composition, treated in a somewhat modern manner. There are five sections to the whole work, namely: *Allemande, Courante, Saraband, Gavotte-Musette* and *Gigue.* Pianists, as a rule, select the *Allemande* and *Gavotte,* which are published separately. We will take up these numbers, which are tuneful and effective.

The *Allemande,* in D minor, gives opportunity for the cultivation of broad, sonorous tone and style. We can almost imagine, as we listen to those broken chord figures, double third passages and little turns, that Emmanuel Bach had written it. But no, it is more pompous and grandiloquent, more modern than the music of this son of the great Bach. But it is equal to the Master Bach, for finger development and control. Practice slowly, with firm, even touch, exact phrasing and attention to time-value of the notes. In the end the piece must be played in broad, massive style.

The *Gavotte* is in decided contrast to the *Allemande,* for it is gay and jovial, though perhaps somewhat heavy footed. This effect, however, can be mitigated by playing lightly, though with well articulated touch. Observe the rhythmic accents and use staccato or slapping touch. The second page has much octave work, which closes brilliantly and forcefully. The *Musette* is very subdued and delicate, legato and suave, quite opposite of the jolly *Gavotte.* These pieces are interesting in themselves, and are about the best-known solos of this exponent of modern pianism; he has also put out a set of eight piano pieces and a piano sonata.

ROBERT SCHUMANN, 1810-1856

These *Fantaisies, Op. 16,* were composed in 1838, and form another link in that chain of tone pictures depicting Schumann's struggle to win Clara Wieck for his wife. They are pictures of his mental fluctuation between hope and despair, exalted passion and deep pensiveness. The set was always a favorite of Schumann. In one of his letters to Clara, he says: "I will call it the *Kreisleriana,* and in it you, and one of your ideas play principal parts. I will dedicate it to you—yes to you and to no one else, and you will smile so sweetly when you find yourself reflected again in its pages." Again he writes: "Do sometimes play my *Kreisleriana.* In some parts of it there speaks a veritable wild love, and your life and mine, and many a look of yours is there." In no other work of Schumann is the dualism between the tender, mild Eusebius and the wild, impetuous Florestan (two imaginary characters) more clearly marked. They had already appeared in the *Carneval, Op. 9,* but in the *Kreisleriana* they become even more prominent.

There are eight of these contrasted mood pictures. Let us select a group, choosing Nos. 1, 4, 5, 6, and 8. Later on the whole work may be assimilated; but this group will give an idea of the composer's mental states.

Number 1 reveals a condition of much excitement, perhaps it is a joyous excitement. The onrushing triplets surge up and down the keyboard, in those figure-patterns through which a melody is woven, if rightly accented. The bass is to be made prominent in the first and third sections. The middle portion, in B flat major, is subdued, and must be played softly and tenderly, with lovely tone quality. This is followed by a repetition of the first part.

Number 4 pictures one of those retrospective moods, in which Schumann seems arguing with fate; it becomes more despondent at the close of page one. At the top of second page a happier mood succeeds. Here a lovely theme enters, which should be played with a beautiful legato touch, backed by an accompaniment which is merely a soft murmur of sound. At the last line, however, the old despondency returns; it will not entirely down, in spite of the hopeful spirit of what has gone before. The whole is a lovely tone poem, full of atmosphere and true feeling.

Number 5. Here is the tricksy elf, the spirit of freakish gaiety, which is never far away, even in Schumann's most sad and serious moments. Here it riots through this charming number. The first two pages must be very exactly phrased, clearly articulated and lightly tossed off, to give the right

effect.   Following this are over two pages of a more
lyric character, touching a deeper note of feeling.
A big crescendo is created on the second page of
this section, where much rhythmic control is necessary to keep the forces well in hand.   This is followed by a return of the themes which occupied
the first portion of the piece.

Number 6.   In this we find another mood of in-
trospection, or retrospection.   Strong contrasts of
light and shade are here; the sky is overcast, with
short passionate outbursts.   A gentler mood enters
at the change of rhythm; the last line has a return
of the first theme in a more resigned spirit.

Number 8 is light and free—a happy mood, beginning softly and moving swiftly.   On page two,
the octaves in the bass must be prominent.   At the
fourth page we have a passage extending to the
middle of page following, which is full of life and
vigor.   It is marked to be played "with all power,"
and seems to be a very weighty pronouncement,
with heavy accents and much pedal.   Study carefully the pedal effects in this and in all the pieces
of the set.   The effort to assimilate the meaning of
these poetical pieces, and to deliver it with variety
of touch and tone, will be of vital benefit to the
player.

SCRIABINE, 1871-1915

This Russian composer has been a most interesting figure in the world of music.   So highly gifted

that he could play a piece on the piano as a child of eight after but once hearing, and play it perfectly on through the achievements of a short but productive life, prove him to have been a musical genius of high order. He passed through various stages of development; his later compositions are somewhat strange and mystical, while his earlier piano pieces are cast in the mold of Chopin, whose music he adored, though he strove not to imitate what he so greatly admired.

One of the best examples of his earlier style is the *Nocturne, Op. 9, No. 2, in D flat,* for left hand alone; it is the first example we have used of pieces for one hand. Students often require extra work for the left hand, though with proper study both hands should become equally developed. However, if no extra effort for the left hand is needed, the Scriabine Nocturne is melodious, unusual, and will well repay study.

The principle to be observed in rendering "one-hand" music, is to make it sound as though played in the usual way, with both hands; the listener, with eyes closed, should not detect any difference. In a piece of lyric character, the three parts, melody, bass and accompaniment, must preserve their respective places in the tonal scheme, and not encroach on each other.

The melody of the *Nocturne* is played with arm weight, which should develop a rich, warm tone quality. When the melody and accompaniment

come together, the one must *sing,* the other be subdued.   Broken chords carry the melody on their
top notes.   Preserve the rhythm and the melodic
line of the theme, as it rises and falls, through careful tone shadings.   At the top of the second page
a more strenuous portion enters, which rises to a
climax at the *fortissimo,* and dies down to a murmur at the *cadenza,* which should be played very
legato.   After this episode the main themes are repeated, with a few changes, and a second cadenza
closes the piece.   The trills here must be smooth and
flowing.   We are again reminded how necessary
it is to practice trills in our technic study, trills in
all keys, with each pair of fingers in turn and with
each hand separately, as well as with both together.
The pedal plays an especially important and indis-
pensable part in this piece, as it must in all left-
hand music, and its intelligent, artistic use will
greatly aid both tone and interpretation.

RACHMANINOFF, 1873-

The great Russian composer-pianist, at present
a resident of America, has composed a goodly number of Preludes, outside of the very familiar one
in C sharp minor.   One of these Preludes which is
fast becoming popular with pianists, is the one we
have chosen—in G minor.   As played by Josef
Hofmann, who first introduced it to American
audiences, it is an inspiring dance, with marked

rhythm and a flowing lyric middle movement. Played by Prokofieff, the fiery Russian pianist-composer, it is a rushing torrent, that carries all before it like a whirlwind.

The first two pages have such an infectious rhythmic swing, that one almost unconsciously taps the foot in sympathetic response. This rhythmic pulse must be brought out in the playing. Practice slowly, with well-marked staccato touch, and with the necessary accents; then work up with metronome.

The middle section expresses a beautiful theme, and should be smooth and flowing, also very legato, in spite of some awkward stretches and intervals. Bring out the melody above the accompaniment, even though it tries to hide itself behind other notes.

A connecting passage leads to the return of the first portion of the piece, which can now be dashed off with even more bravoura than at first.

Love Dream Number 3. Liszt seemed to have a special leaning toward writing lyric music overlaid with many accompanying figures and arabesques, or to take well-known songs or opera airs and dress them up with many ornaments and *fioriture*. Think of the many songs of Schubert and even by Schumann which he has translated into effective piano solos. Liszt was without doubt the greatest piano virtuoso of his time; he could work wonders—people said even miracles—with the instrument. He could also write with as much piano-effectiveness as he could play. It has become the fashion in some quarters to belittle the compositions of Liszt and his contribution to the literature of the piano. But if we take away the rhapsodies, concertos, B minor Sonata, transcriptions and other solos, the piano world would suffer a real loss.

The *Love Dreams* are three original lyric compositions for piano, based on German poems. Only the third of these seems to be used, though the first, with poem by Uhland, is well made, and the second is a short, passionate love scene, yet number 3 is always chosen. The poem exhorts to unselfish love for the beloved, with no harsh word or act to be regretted when it is too late. The melody is one of those poignantly expressive themes which Liszt, always seeking for the intense and gripping, has been able to catch and reproduce at the keyboard.

The theme should sound as though played on the 'cello. To this end it is advised to use the *left* hand for the melody, even though this means breaking the interval when it is more than an octave. For if the theme is divided between the two hands, as most editions have it, the effect of continuity is not so likely to be attained, for the tones have not always the same quality and may not stand out with the same roundness and sonority. Color the eight tones before the first cadenza, by making a slight *sostenuto-crescendo*. The cadenza in right hand can be fingered 24, 1-3, 5-2, 1-3 and so on. Toward the close preserve the rhythm of 3.

From this point on, the movement becomes more agitated and impassioned. At change of key the big chords in right hand are sounded with increasing power and stress; the whole fourth page is a climax of dramatic intensity, which calms and cools in the chromatic figures of the second cadenza. This must be played with crystalline delicacy, until it dies away at the end in little exhausted sighs, simulated by lifting the hand after each of the last pairs of notes.

As if worn with the ecstasy of passionate feeling, the first *Tempo* returns quietly. The movement becomes slower, the tone softer and more dreamy. The first measure in arpeggio leads to celestial harmonies; play them in this spirit. Study the tone quality until you obtain the effect you seek. The last eight measures form a short *Coda,* and seem an afterthought, tucked on for no especial reason; only beautiful, silvery tones can make it seem logical.

Many players attempt this third *Love Dream* only to injure it, through lack of right conditions of arm and hand. The aim must be to create beautiful tone quality with every note, colored with all possible variety. The piece begins quietly, rises to the heights of emotion, then subsides—goes out as it came in—quietly. But it can be made to express a world of emotion with great tonal variety, in the hands of a sympathetic and resourceful player.

Rhapsodie, Number 4. The "torrent of splendor," which Liszt has called Hungarian Rhapsodie Number 4, is not one of those frequently heard, but it deserves to be better known. There are fifteen Rhapsodies. Some have been worn threadbare, as the Second and Sixth or even the Twelfth, while others are still new and fresh, waiting the practiced hand and sympathetic thought to reveal their beauties. For there are many emotional and sympathetic strains in these compositions; they are not all froth and fury, as some believe. Paderewski is one great artist who has always spoken in high terms of this music, and he interprets it with the greatest insight and mastery. Those who used to listen to his interpretation of the 2nd, 6th and 10th, will never forget the thrilling experience.

The *Fourth Rhapsodie* is shorter than those already mentioned. It is somewhat new to the public. The opening phrases are grandiloquent. Take the first three notes with third finger and arm-weight touch. From 5th to 8th measures, the mood is lyric and singing, with melody brought forward and accompaniment light and subdued. Now come heavy octaves, played with body weight and alternating with measures of crisp delicacy.

Three lines of second page again flare up imposingly, but taper down softly to the cadenza. Here the left hand pronounces a melody àgainst the tracery of the treble. The closing portion must be emphatically bravoura, with a ritard leading to closing measure, in true Hungarian refrain.

At the *Andantino* a second theme enters, more restless and wild than the first. After this comes another of contrasting character, dainty and capricious, and flowering in a cadenza. This last is repeated, ending in another cadenza, somewhat longer, which brings the first half of the *Rhapsodie* to a close.

Octave passages make up the remainder; these form a continuous melody. Various fine effects can be made in these four pages. The theme is tossed back and forth from one hand to another, to be played now delicately, now powerfully. To those who find octaves comparatively easy, there will be no great difficulty in working up these passages. For small hands the effort will be much greater. But there is hardly a piece I know of, outside of the *Sixth Rhapsodie,* or the big Chopin *Polonaise Op. 53,* that will be of more value as a study of octaves. Keep this movement in your repertoire and play it daily—for years; your technic will reap great benefit.

PART TWO

NUMBER I

REQUEST LESSONS

During a long association with *The Musical Observer,* I established a department known as "The New Round Table." The aim of this department was to prove a sort of meeting place for teachers of piano, young pianists and even parents, where each and all could bring their particular problems and difficulties to be lightened and solved, as the case might be.

There is no need here to refer to the many letters received—some full of mystifying ignorance, others requesting specific assistance, others again expressing cordial, encouraging approval. One class of writers desired assistance on pieces. Their intelligent questions proved they were eager for more light on compositions they were studying by themselves. It was a pleasure to lend a helping hand to such earnest students, often living at great distance from a music centre, and therefore unable to attend piano recitals or hear much music of any kind.

It may be that the letters sent to these inquiring ones, through the medium of the "New Round

Table," may be helpful to a wider circle of workers. In this hope I have included them in the present volume.

Request Lesson Number 1: Bach, *Prelude and Fugue, C sharp major* (Well Tempered Clavichord, Book 1, No. 3).

"I am trying to learn the *C sharp major Prelude and Fugue* of Bach, and would like some help on the technic and interpretation, especially of the Prelude." R. P.

The *Third Prelude,* from the Well Tempered Clavichord, is Bach in one of his happiest, gayest moods. The little piece fairly laughs and bubbles with merriment before our very eyes—and ears. William H. Sherwood, the American pianist, used to find in it a suggestion of two little ballet dancers —not a group, but just two, who alternate their figures. First one little dancer comes out and does a *pas seul,* then falls back and the other takes her place. The character of the Prelude bears out this pretty conceit, for it is full of sprightly gaiety. How can anyone imagine Bach's music to be dry and uninteresting, when it expresses every emotion that can be thought or felt, all the way from grave to gay! This Prelude belongs to the happy side of life, and should be played in the spirit of joyous brightness.

Now, by what means shall this effect be achieved? A light, crisp touch must be used, together with a reasonable amount of swiftness. This effect may be created through three distinct qualities of touch and tone production, which the player will do well to develop. The well-equipped pianist and teacher is one who has studied with various masters, in order to arrive at just this catholicity of utterance on the piano. No one master or method has all the truth there is in piano playing. After arriving at a certain stage of technical and musical proficiency (not before, mind you!), we must be many-sided, gathering ideas from many sources.

Touch Number One. The first way in which the Prelude may be practiced is with well-defined finger action. The hand is held in arched position while fingers preserve stroke position, when unemployed. The fingers act in curved position and a pure legato touch should be the result. This touch would doubtless be used exclusively by a pianist who has been trained in the German or Viennese school of mechanism; it is a good, solid, fundamental manner of tone production, and would probably be the normal touch with most players when beginning the study of this Prelude, or of Bach in general.

Touch Number Two. We may use the so-called elastic, or drawing-off touch in this Prelude with good effect. The elastic touch was a specialty of Dr. William Mason, who learned the principles of it from Liszt. The touch in question is executed by drawing each finger, as it plays, over the surface of the key towards the palm of the hand. It is claimed for the drawing-off movement that it lightens up touch and tone, rendering both less sticky and heavy, and producing a clear, brilliant—though not powerful—quality of tone. The elastic touch can be used with good result in the study of the Prelude, for the student learns thereby to articulate the tones with clarity and precision.

Touch Number Three. A very modern method of playing delicate passage work, is by employing a light, rebounding action of fingers, acting from knuckle joints. The fingers are held in a somewhat straightened position, while making the necessary light taps or slaps upon the keys. When facility is gained through use of this touch and the required movements, one feels almost no effort while playing; the fingers seem to go of themselves. Practise very slowly at first, giving special attention to the passages of sixteenth notes. These light movements become so effortless that the keys almost seem to play of themselves; the keys seem to lift the fingers up and off, after the light taps are given. This is the French manner of playing rapid, light passages, and it certainly has ease, grace and elegance to recommend it. The expression "shake the notes out of your sleeve" must have been applied to some such touch as this, for it is the essence of articulated lightness.

It is suggested to practice the Prelude with touch number one first, before trying the others.

After a thorough study of the Prelude with these touches, or especially using the first and last, let us go over the Prelude for a few points of interpretation.

In the edition edited by Franz Kroll, which was especially recommended by Von Bülow, the third Prelude and Fugue are written in D flat, instead of in C sharp, as in other editions. This particular edition has fingering but no marks of expression.

Begin the Prelude *piano;* in fact there are no great dynamic contrasts used in these two pages. The fascinating turns and steps of the little dancers are of sufficient interest without seeking for exaggerated tone color. Play it simply, with buoyant yet delicate tone and clear, released touch—avoiding all stiffness and heaviness.

As the eight measure sequences ascend, they will naturally increase somewhat in stress. There are four of these sequences, after which comes a working out passage of about sixteen measures. Then the first theme returns, for two repetitions. From here on to the end the phrases are more or less detached, with alternate movements between the hands, to be played lightly, with semi-detached touch. Here there can be more tonal light and shade, made with little crescendos and diminuendoes, and with a somewhat broadening of tone at the end.

Dr. William Mason considered this Prelude an excellent daily exercise for smoothness, evenness and control. "Whenever you have five minutes to spare," he used to say, "while waiting for a friend, or on coming in from a walk, just sit down and play the *Prelude in C-sharp;* it will refresh you."

The Fugue, like the Prelude, is in the same happy vein. It is written in but three voices, and the theme or text occupies the two opening measures.

The student will make a study of the theme, and then proceed to analyze the Fugue, in order to discover how many repetitions of the theme can be found in the two pages. In its entirety there are about ten, though one can find several places where the theme appears only in half statements.

The great point in fugue playing is to understand the theme thoroughly and to bring it out above the other parts. In this way the fugue is a continuous song, sung by different voices—the notes not belonging to the theme forming a tonal background to the whole. These secondary voices must be kept in the background or else they will interfere with the flow of the principal song.

The question of making a ritard at the close of a Bach fugue has often been discussed, with many pros and cons. The reason for this ritard is found in the fact that the organs of Bach's time, for which many of the fugues were written, were rather small affairs. As the fugue always became more complicated at the close, using more power and usually more notes, this required more wind and more strength to pump it in; hence the necessity of the ritard.

When the C-sharp major Fugue is well studied with legato touch, apply the rebounding touch to the lighter passages.

NUMBER II

SONATA PATHETIQUE, BEETHOVEN

Almost all the great composers were child prodigies; think of Bach, Mozart, Mendelssohn, Chopin, Liszt, to mention only a few. Naturally Beethoven was a prodigy, though not of the exotic sort, like Mozart or Chopin. We have his own words that "From my fourth year, music has been my favorite pursuit." He must have loved music to the very core of his being, but, it seems, he hated the routine of practice, as it was presented to him in those early years. However, he was obliged to learn piano and violin, as his father was a strict taskmaster. When quite a lad he was organist at the Elector's Court, in his home town of Bonn, and later played viola in the Court Orchestra. Thus he learned practical lessons from two of the greatest instruments, organ and orchestra. This early training must surely have given color and power to his piano compositions. In his great symphonies he speaks as an inspired orator, uplifting his hearers; through the medium of the piano he reveals himself. He confides to the piano his secret joys, sorrows, love, hope, despair, exaltation; but through these varied emotions he is always simple and sincere, with no straining after false effects.

A writer on Beethoven remarks that his piano music requires sound and solid execution. Then he goes on to say that the principal conditions are a powerful yet gentle touch, with the greatest possible independence of finger. Therefore the sonatas should not be placed in hands uneducated for their reception. When that degree of progress has been attained which can master technical difficulties, the enjoyment to be derived from their thorough study will be doubled, and the effort to grasp their inner meaning will not be held back by immature preparation.

Beethoven's figures and forms are built on scales, chords and arpeggios, reminding us of the Czerny-Clementi school of technic (Beethoven was a pupil of Czerny). But this is only the outward semblance of the inner meaning. For we know the master infused into those mechanical forms a rich emotional vitality, in which almost every shade of feeling can be discovered, waiting to be revealed by the properly trained fingers of the player, guided by his sympathetic comprehension of the meaning of the music.

Before beginning the study of the *Sonata Pathétique,* the player has undoubtedly become somewhat familiar with Beethoven's manner in the two sonatinas Op. 49; also in the Sonata Op. 2, No. 1, the *Op. 14, in G major,* and perhaps the three comprising Op. 10. The three sonatas Op. 10 may be considered of equal technical difficulty, though not so charged with emotion as Op. 13. It is not advisable to plunge into the *Pathétique* before some such preparation has been made. We have all, doubtless at some moment of our lives, been forced to listen maybe to an immature girl, who, with no conception of the meaning of what she is playing, attempts to perform, in true salon style, the Sonata we are considering. The *Pathétique* is a work fraught with profound intellectual and emotional meaning. It is full of passion, now gloomy, now gay—tender and bright by turns. It requires thorough study, both on the technical and interpretative sides.

With music on the desk of the piano before you, a few suggestions will be offered for the study and performance of this great work. To be really helpful, these suggestions must take up technical terms and points, the necessary movements of arms and fingers, with ideas for shading and phrasing. Only in this way will correct effects be produced.

Sonata Pathétique, Beethoven (Edition Klindworth).

Introduction. Grave: First chord *forte,* second beat, *piano,* swelling to third beat; fourth beat soft, short. Second measure the same. Third measure, accent on first and third, short swells on second and fourth beats. Fourth measure, cadenza, played with clear finger action, with increasing followed by diminishing tone. Fifth measure *piano,* with octaves well bound, and fourth beat *ff,* taken with heavy arm weight.   Sixth measure the same.   At eighth measure begin a gradual *crescendo*, leading to first chord, ninth measure.   Here the sixteenths are light and non-legato.   The same in tenth measure. Eleventh measure accent second sixteenth and descend the scale passage with great velocity, smoothness and brilliancy.

It is a good plan to play the Introduction with the metronome at 66 to an eighth, counting eight beats in a measure; this will render the time and rhythm very exact.

Allegro, with metronome at 144 to a half note.

Prepare fingers for each interval found in right hand.   Use marcato touch, with combined wrist and arm movement.   Small *crescendo* begins at second measure; a larger one at fifth measure, falling off at the end of seventh measure.   Descending runs at 19th and 23rd measures must be clear and flowing.   Strong accents on octaves at 21st and 32nd measures.   At 25th measure begins the upward figures, found again at 29th, 30th and 33rd measures.   Use prepared fingers, arm movements and crescendos for each one.   At the 47th measure begin the mordents.   Finger them 2-4-3, and make them crisp and quick, though they are often played as triplets and more slowly.   At the 79th measure a gradual *crescendo* begins, which culminates at the 89th-90th measures.   Bring out the upper melody and subdue inner parts in both hands.   At the 103rd measure, accent the high E flat, also the octave E flat, four measures ahead, and work up a *crescendo* to the double bar. The *Interlude* of four measures is played like the *Introduction*.

Beginning again to number the continuation of the Allegro, in E minor, we find an octave half note in fifth measure to be played with arm weight, but lightened when the arm is lifted at the F sharp. All the pairs are played in the same way. Watch the Left Hand phrasing, beginning at 13th measure. The two little rumbling passages, measures 31-35, and 39-42, are to be very soft and even, with triumphant soaring figures between. At measure 59, the theme returns in C minor, after a long descending passage. What was said in the first instance, applies to the finishing of the movement. Much clearness, applied to touch and phrasing, is necessary all through; fingers prepared for chords, accents in the right places—rhythmic certainty. The dots over the eighth note figures, such as those over passages beginning at 83rd measure, Part One, and others of the same nature, only indicate slight detachment and stress, not staccato, in the exact meaning of the term.

Adagio, metronome at 60 for an eighth note.

This movement is in regular form, that is to say, first four measures ending on the dominant, the next four on the tonic. In the calm, satisfying key of A flat, the Movement is a beautiful example of melody and accompaniment in the same hand. The melody, in a singing legato, perfectly connected, should rise above a subdued accompaniment. At measure 17, the second subject enters. Play Left Hand with combined wrist and arm movement. The turn in measure 20, comes with the sixth chord in bass. At 37th measure, a third theme enters. The melody *legato,* with subdued accompaniment, and combined movements. This combined movement is to be used right along, until the accompanying figure changes, at 51st measure. Here we have one *legato* and two *staccato* notes to each beat, with sustained melody above them. The *Coda* enters at 66th measure. At measures 70-71-72, accent third beats, diminishing the whole until the end.

Rondo, metronome at 96 for a half note.

In working up the *Rondo,* it would be well to put the metronome at, say 72-80 and so on up to 144, for a quarter note. Then try 60-80 to a half note. Make the whole movement crisp and clean, with exact phrasing, distinct legato and staccato and exact rhythm and accents. Naturally the metronome aids this rhythmic exactness. Have fingers well curved for chords. For the places marked with trills, five notes are sufficient. Practice scales with finger *staccato,* in order to render the *staccato* passages with clearness and precision. Also give great attention to dynamics.

When you have done all these things, you will be ready—and it is hoped—able to apprehend and also achieve the interpretation of this wonderful Sonata.

NUMBER III

EDWARD GRIEG, NOCTURNE

How often we players and teachers bless the composers who give us worthy music in small forms! Schumann, the master, set the example; MacDowell and Grieg followed in his steps. They were all writers of lovely pieces—real musical miniatures, which are greatly esteemed by pianists, indeed by all who love music. These short pieces, depicting a picture or mood, open the door to self expression for many who would not or could not attempt a more lengthy composition. One or two pages may be tolerably mastered, where six or eight might require too sustained concentration to memorize and perfect. This is not to imply that the shorter piece is lacking in pith and meaning, for it may have more of these qualities—it may have more depth of meaning than the lengthy one. It may say much in little. At all events it usually speaks in simple form, and in language which is easy of comprehension; it speaks to the heart. There are not apt to be long, involved musical phrases and drawn-out passages, since there is no time for these in the brief, intense composition.

And first a word about the music of the North. "In Norwegian music," says Professor Spaulding, "we find the exhuberant rhythmic vitality, typical of a people living in the bold and highly-colored scenery of that sun-lit land. Grieg, a born lyric poet, saturated with folk-music, has embodied this spirit in his compositions. Most of his work is in miniature, and is the expression—like the music of Schubert and Chopin—of moods, short and intense. While Grieg's music is patterned upon Norwegian folk-dances and folk-melodies, it is something far more. He has evolved from the characteristics of his native land a bold, original harmony, and a power of color and description thoroughly his own. In fact Grieg was the first popular impressionist, and for his influence in humanizing and freeing his art from academic routine, his fame will endure."

Grieg has been called by von Bülow, the Chopin of the North, while D. G. Mason says of his music: "It is intimate, suggestive, intangible. It voices the gentlest feelings of the heart, or summons up the airiest visions of the imagination. It is whimsical too, changes its hues like the chameleon and often surprises us with a sudden flight to some unexpected shade of expression. Again, its *finesse* is striking. The phrases are polished like gems, the melodies charm us with their perfect proportions, the cadences are as consummate as they are novel."

In *To the Spring,* and in the *Nocturne,* to mention two of the loveliest of Grieg's short pieces, we find the little problem of uneven rhythms, the two against three forms. The player who would deliver these uneven forms with smoothness and exactness must be able to do so outside the piece, by mastering special exercises in such forms.

The subject of irregular rhythms is one much neglected by piano students in general. If they have a group or short passage of uneven notes in a piece, they manage to get through it some way, contented to do it passably and let it go at that. But to execute a continuous passage in irregular rhythm seems an impossibility. Uneven rhythms of two against three or three against four should not be left to guesswork; they require a perfectly logical elucidation. Begin with a slow trill in each hand, playing two notes in one hand to three in the other. The second note of the pair must be played exactly between the second and third notes of the triplet, but without displacing the rhythm. A brief illustration will demonstrate this more clearly. Count six for each beat containing the triplets. The first note of this and of the pair in the other hand, will go to count One. At count Three is played the second note of the triplet; at Four the second note of the pair; at Five the third note of the triplet. In this way you have the whole problem in a nutshell. Practice this as a continuous exercise, with each pair of fingers in turn; afterwards in scale forms, not only with two's against three's but with three's against four's. With such preparation no irregular rhythms can disturb you in any composition.

Grieg's *Nocturne, Op. 54, No. 5*—the only Nocturne the composer ever wrote, is a lovely tone poem, full of tender feeling and sentiment. Technically it presents no great difficulty, outside of the rhythmical problem already spoken of, which needs deter anyone, almost, from learning it. The piece requires sympathetic touch, beautiful tone production, taste and style in the interpretation. The melody must be made to speak, to sing—to voice the story of sweet, adoring confidence which it seems to embody. The accompaniment is to be subdued yet sufficiently in evidence to support the theme. This support should be delivered with something of the rotary arm movement, which should be applied generally to all chordal accompaniments to prevent them from becoming stiff, heavy and labored.

The very first note in bass, played with arm weight by right hand, arrests attention; it is at once continued by the chromatic phrase in left hand, which should be *legato,* while the accompanying thirds are to be light and detached.

Soon the principal melody enters, a tender, passionate strain, rising and falling like heart throbs. At the beginning of second page the mood changes —or rather the song of love is hushed for a moment, as we listen to the song of birds, trilling their happy airs among the leafy glades of the garden. Is it not the nightingale's voice we hear, pouring out those clear, enchanting trills, which begin so magically soft, then grow in tone and rapidity as they proceed? Who can withstand the spell of the night with its perfume, its stars, its flowers, its bird notes, its enchantments! The music increases in power and feeling; then it breaks off, begins softly, again increasing in tone and *tempo*, until a very ecstasy of emotion is reached, and a mighty *crescendo* ascends from the lower to the higher part of the keyboard. This is the dramatic climax of the piece. It can be made more vivid and effective if the left hand plays this ascending passage with detached arm weight movements, rather than with *legato* touch, as indicated in the music.

The ecstasy has spent itself and we return, at top of third page, to the quiet of the opening theme. It is a relief to be soothed by its sweet tenderness, after the restless surging of the second page.

The melody rises and falls as before, pulsing with deep feeling. This time it rises to a greater height of expression than was the case at first. Note the beautiful harmonies which accompany the melody as it recedes, as it sinks back after its climax. Make this portion effective through lovely tone, delicate shading and correct pedalling. The pedal all through the piece must be used with artistic care; there should be enough to support the melody, but not to cover it or blur the harmonies.

Again the voice of birds in the fragrant dusk, twittering and trilling. Grieg loved the birds; his studio was set among great trees, where the feath-ered songsters were fond of making their nests. He has used the bird voices in this love song with rare and sensitive feeling. The impression is of something exotic, not of the earth earthly. These little trills are the final echoes of the poetic mood, and as they die away, we have the long broken chord, whose soft, lingering tones closes this lovely picture.

* See programme No. 5 for further remarks on the Grieg Nocturne.

NUMBER IV

One of the interesting pieces which finds its way into the repertoire of pianists of moderate attainments, is the D flat Romance of Jean Sibelius, and we have been asked to devote one of the request lessons to suggestions on the study and performance of this piece. A composition which contains variety without diffuseness or meaningless repetition, which has expressive melody and is not too long, is greatly in demand by the ambitious amateur, young artist and teacher. The Sibelius Romance is an excellent example of all these favorable qualities, and has endeared itself to many players.

The music has an old-world atmosphere, and calls up to the mind of the player possessing imagination, pictures of the age-old time of Druids, Scalds or other peoples of the Northland. In listening to it we can picture a great hall where princes and warriors often foregather, and imposing functions are frequently held. It is night. Soft lights blossom from the many candelabra that swing low from lofty beams of the ceiling. Priceless tapestries hang upon the walls, rich furs are scattered over the floors. In the great fireplace huge logs are burn-

123

ing, adding their crimson glow to the radiance of the many candles. About the fire are grouped luxurious chairs and settles. In one of the former half reclines a slender slip of a girl, belonging to a princely race. Hers is the strange, delicate beauty of the North, the floating, golden locks, bound by a simple fillet; the fair, rose-tinted skin; flower-blue eyes; supple figure, clad in soft, white robes, gold-bordered.

On a low hassock at her feet is a youthful warrior, fair to look upon, brave, courtly, handsome, a very Prince indeed. They are lovers, and the music voices to a degree, their joys and anxieties. For he must leave his White Dove on the morrow, as his army waits. This final hour is all their own. It is portentous; it may be for the last time; for who can tell what may befall ere they can be together again as now.

Having some such mental picture in mind we may be able to make the Romance more real and vital. One feels at once that this is descriptive music. This being felt, the player is then at liberty to form his own concept, paint his own picture. But a picture of some sort he may easily imagine, though it may not be along the exact line here suggested.

Of Jean Sibelius the man and his personality we know not a great deal, except what is revealed in his music. He is indeed the greatest of Finnish composers. With him, as with Schumann, music stood higher than law. Sent to Helsingfors in

1885, at the age of twenty, to become a lawyer, he abandoned his studies at the end of the first semester and entered the Conservatory. After eight years of close study, he was appointed teacher of composition at the Conservatory. His first published compositions attracted such favorable attention that the Finnish Senate granted him an annual sum equal to six hundred dollars for ten years. In 1900 he accompanied his native Philharmonic Orchestra on a European tour, conducting many of his own works. His art rests on folk music, and his original themes contain all the characteristics of real folk melodies. He has composed five symphonies, various other symphonic pieces, an opera, much chamber music, about fifty remarkable songs, a piano sonata and other pieces for the instrument. The charming Romance we shall now study is perhaps the best known.

Those softly murmuring tonic triads, which fill the first two measures of the Romance, are simple enough in themselves to be played by almost a tyro. But touch and tone are everything here, to create the necessary atmosphere, to anticipate the mood. We feel their quiet and calm, in which there is a touch of expectancy, awaiting what is to follow. In playing these opening measures, fingers must be held with reasonable firmness, and should retain their shape for the two chord positions. The chords are played with a somewhat detached touch, slight rotary hand movements and relaxed arm. Start deliberately; a sense of hurry would fatally mar the effect. I have heard this piece ruined at the very outset by a hasty, ill-considered delivery of these two measures.

The song or theme in left hand, enters at third measure. First of all make yourself familiar with this theme. Play it alone until something of its haunting charm, its moving appeal grips you. To make this yearning quality of tone, you well know you must employ arm weight—absolute unrestricted freedom of arm. Little or no pedal need be used for the three measures of 'cello-like melody (the man's voice) but pedal is held through the following measure. This measure is marked *pianissimo.* The theme is now exactly repeated, but the resourceful player will slightly vary the tonal values.

And now begins another portion of the melody, higher up—the woman's voice, and her song-speech is a counterpart of her lover's. She has a passage of eight measures, which closes on the tonic. A little flutter of excitement now arises, with those pairs of single tones; the sound increases to *forte,* with a couple of *sforzando* chords, which must stand out. At the end of this short passage, the second theme, or woman's voice, recurs, this time joined to the man's voice in a lovely duet of about four measures (see passage in thirds). A connecting passage of three measures, *accellerando,* leads to a brief return of the first theme, and the manly voice is heard again above the soft murmur of the

girl's part. Prepare the fingers for this succession
of thirds and sixths; make them even, smooth and
legato.

We now reach the tonic chord and start, as it
were, afresh. The outlook is broader; big chords
accompany the first, or 'cello theme; there is some
unrest, a reminder that duty calls, a vision of what
the morrow may bring, the inevitable separation
from the beloved, even if only for a short time.
Then, at the *dolce,* her voice is heard, softly persuasive, alluring, endearing. Remember the soprano theme should be phrased in figures of six
notes, and the hand-arm lifted between. This applies to the passage whenever it appears, from first
to last. The lover soon adds his voice to hers—in
the double thirds—and both sing the lovely melody
together. The player can make a tonal contrast
between the six note figure beginning on A flat and
C, and the lower one, beginning on E and G.

From here to the end of the scale, following the
cadenza, all is excitement. The young warrior
describes the coming onslaught on the enemy, the
struggle, the final victory, when the pennons are
borne aloft to the heights in triumph. Those big,
full-blooded chords describe graphically the hoped-
for victory. This chord passage must be delivered
with full, sonorous tone quality, with heavy arm
weight, and pedal for each chord. The power lapses
toward the close of the eight measures, and ends
in a soft cadence of two chords.

Then the girl's voice is heard in her own particular theme—so appealing, so expressive. She has absolute faith in her stalwart warrior, her noble and brave Prince. He will realize her high hopes, he will win a great victory; he will return to her unscathed and unharmed. She is sure of this, therefore she is content. They can enjoy this blessed hour together without fear of what the future may hold for them.

The shadows deepen in the great hall, as the lights burn low; the firelight casts fitful rosy gleams upon the earnest young faces; all is strangely still; they can almost hear the beating of their own hearts. All is peace and calm.

As you study and play this charming number, endeavor to invest it with the atmosphere of romance, through your soulful touch, variety of nuance, tonal shading and artistic conception.

NUMBER V

CHOPIN, PRELUDE IN D FLAT

The Preludes of Chopin are the pianist's most treasured possession, the one work of the great Pole he would be most loath to part with. In this wonderful collection there are found utterances reflecting every mood, now grave now gay, both long and difficult or very brief, as the shortest consists of but a couple of lines. The Preludes are beloved by artist and amateur alike. They seem to be adapted to all classes of pianists. The player who has lately started on the path, if he have serious aims and poetic thought, can cope with the easy numbers, while the longer and more intricate ones are suited to the powers of the advanced pianist.

Many writers have discussed on these favorite pieces. Ehlert says: "No work of Chopin portrays his inner organization so faithfully and completely. One finds in them the thunderous power of the *Scherzi*, the half satirical, half coquettish elegance of the *Mazurkas*, together with the southern luxuriance and fragrant breath of the *Nocturnes*. Often it is as though they were small falling stars, dissolving into flowers as they fall."

The *Prelude in D flat, No. 15*, is one of the most

familiar. It is thought Georges Sand referred to it when she wrote of the Preludes: "Some of them create such vivid impressions that the shades of dead monks seem to rise in solemn and gloomy funereal pomp."

The work needs no programme. Its serene beginning, lugubrious interlude, with the dominant pedal never ceasing in a *basso ostinato,* gives color to Kleczynski's idea that the *B minor Prelude, No. 6,* is a sketch of the idea which is elaborated in No. 15.   In describing the latter, he says:

"The foundation of the picture is the drops of rain constantly falling, which by their continual patter bring the mind to a state of sadness.   A melody full of tears is heard through the rush of the rain; then passing to the key of C sharp minor, it rises from the depths of the bass to a prodigious *crescendo,* indicative of the terror which nature, in its deathly aspects, excites in the heart of man." To Niecks the C sharp minor portion affects one as in an oppressive dream.   "The entrance, or rather re-entrance of the D flat section, which dispels the dreadful nightmare, comes upon one with the smiling freshness of dear, familiar nature."

Another version of the story pictures Chopin at home alone, at night, communing with his piano, his friends having left him for the evening.   The house where he is staying is an old castle, or monastery, with great lonely rooms and echoing corridors.   The sensitive poet-musician feels the chill and gloom of his surroundings and has taken refuge with his beloved instrument. A storm outside sends the rain beating monotonously against the casement. The continuous drip of the rain begins to tell on the frail man's nerves. He fancies a troop of warriors are approaching; they come nearer and nearer; in another moment they will be upon him, will trample him under their horses' hoofs. He is wrought to a frenzy, and only by a supreme effort does he conquer his terror. As the first theme returns, his friends enter and find him.

Mr. Alfred Cortot, the eminent French pianist, gives his idea of this Prelude as follows:

"A young mother rocking her child—she is half asleep herself. A frightful nightmare shows her the scaffold which is waiting for her son. While the awakening dispels her hallucinations, it leaves her still disquieted."

For the opening D flat section of the Prelude, an atmosphere must prevail. The movements are slow and creeping, with relaxed arm weight. In the left hand the tones of longer duration are naturally a little more prominent, with a small *crescendo* at beginning of third measure. The single tones keep up a regular undertow of monotonous tone, which has suggested the dropping of rain. This is monotonous only in being regular, for it fluctuates in tone quality with the theme. We have considered the meaning of the music from a pictorial, poetic, emotional viewpoint. It should be played in such a way as to produce the suave, song-like character of the nocturne, the storm and stress of the C sharp minor section, and the calm and peace of the return to the final portion. The player needs a sympathetic touch, variety of tone quality, command of dynamic gradation—from very soft to *fortissimo,* all performed with beautiful, melting tone, deep and full without harshness, subdued, yet with carrying quality.

The first eight measures contain two phrases of the lovely penetrating melody, played entirely legato. Build the phrase through a gradual increase to the G flat, then a slight falling off in tone. At the ninth the second portion of the song-theme appears. It has a couple of repetitions, with exquisite little grace note groups. A connecting measure brings a return of the first theme, played twice, and leading to the portentous C sharp minor section.

This middle section, in C sharp minor, still contains the raindrop theme, but it now consists of G sharps. These insistent tones are detached very slightly, played with arm weight, and a wrist that yields for each note. It is the bass that carries the melody or theme, and marches relentlessly forward, like oncoming fate. These twelve measures —to the double bar—resolve themselves into three groups of four measures each; the first group very soft, with little shadings, the next group louder, with strong accents, and the final group *fortissimo,* with heavy, relaxed arm weight. Continuing after the double bar, the right hand takes part in the theme building, though not with such ponderous weight as before. In the final measure of this section, Cortot broke the right hand chords slightly. The measure which effects a return to the first theme and change of key, should be played much slower and softer.

It is with a sense of relief from the strain of the weird minor section, that we welcome the reappearance of the first theme. Hofmann and Cortot paint these concluding lines in shadowy tints, beginning *pianissimo*. After the fourth measure a ritard sets in. The tones of the two-measure passage in simple notes should be colored by touchmoulding, for these measures are significant. After this all dies down, becoming softer and softer to the end. When De Pachman plays it he makes the raindrops appear to melt into thin air, and become well-nigh inaudible.

The D flat Prelude seems a "rose between two abysses," since it is preceded by the "Stormy Sea," as Cortot calls No. 14, and followed by "The Road to the Abyss," No. 16 (Cortot). To follow the simile, the rose, so drowsily fragrant as we first grasp it, cannot make us overlook the sharp thorns on its stem. But the thorns are salutary, since they enhance, by contrast, its beauty and fragrance. At the close thorns are forgotten, but beauty and fragrance remain.

NUMBER VI

The only big Polonaise MacDowell wrote he has placed as the final number of the Virtuoso Studies, Op. 46; it is a brilliant example of virility and bravura. As it is both valuable as music and composed by a representative American musician, we have two good reasons for studying it.

A few words about the polonaise form in general may be of interest. We think of the polonaise as a dance, gay and rather wild, a national dance of Poland, and of the Polish composer, Chopin, who made that dance distinctive.

There is a record that the polonaise originated at a royal reception held for the King of Poland, at Cracow, in 1574, at which the nobles and their wives marched past the throne in organized procession, to the strains of rhythmic, stately music. From this time the polonaise gradually became accepted as the opening dance at all court festivities. Perhaps the Polonaise, which in the old days was so full of stateliness, had kinship with the dignified Pavans and Passomezzos which were in vogue at the French Court in the fifteenth century.

The tempo of the polonaise is that of a march, taken at a pace between an Andante and an Allegro,

134

and always begins on the first beat of the measure.

From the middle of the eighteenth century, composers have favored this form of slow, stately dance. Bach wrote several polonaises and a polacca —the Italian term for the word; the *Polacca* occurs in the *Brandenburg Concerto, No. 1.* Haendel left one or two examples, Beethoven several; Mozart included a *Rondeau and Polonaise* in the *Sonata in D minor;* Schubert wrote Polonaises for four hands, Weber a *Polonaise, Op. 21,* and a *Polacca Brilliante, Op. 72.* Then came Chopin, a true Pole, filled with fervent national spirit. He realized the rhythmic possibilities of the polonaise, imbued it with fresh life and energy, changing it from a slow, severe march-form into a glowing, rhythmic tone picture of Poland, her many wrongs, her hoped-for regeneration. Of the eleven compositions in this form left by him, some are martial and militant in spirit, and mirror the feudal Court of Poland in the days of its greatness; others are distinguished by a dreamy melancholy and suggest a picture of the country in its adversity.

The modern idea of the Polonaise is of a dance full of life and movement. Instead of the slow, stately march of the old days, we have a real dance in livelier tempo. But even with quickened tempo, we always encounter the distinctive rhythm belonging to this form of composition.

It is a long step from Chopin's *Polonaise Fantaisie,* for instance, to MacDowell's *Polonaise, Op.*

46. In the former there are many changes of rhythm, tempo and feeling; the prevailing mood is dreamy, even sad. MacDowell's music, on the other hand, is full of life and energy, full of fire and brilliancy. It abounds in sharp contrasts of light and shade—in *pianissimo* alternating with vigorous climaxes. In order to play it with effect one must possess a well-developed technic, firm, flexible fingers, arm weight for heavy chords, good rhythmic sense and variety of touch.

As in much of MacDowell's music, there is an abundance of chords in this piece. Laurence Gilman, speaking of the richness of his chord progressions, says: "I can think of no other composer, save Wagner, whose chord progressions are so full and opulent in color. His tonal web is always densely woven—he avoids *thinness*. In addition to the plangency of his chord combinations, his polyphonic skill is responsible for much of the solidity of his fabric." The same writer remarks in another place: "He has, in an uncommon degree, the intimate, visualizing faculty of the Celt." And the composer himself avowed, a few years before his death, "There is in all my work, the Celtic influence: I love its color and meaning; the development in music of that influence is, I believe, a new field." MacDowell seemed to realize he had the field to himself. He is, strangely enough, the first Celtic influence of genuine importance, which has been exerted on creative music. This Celtic note was sounded in the music of this composer, who had in his make-up so much of the "wisdom of old romance."

In his own individual, inimitable way MacDowell would write a different sort of polonaise from any other composer; it would have much life, vitality, movement; it would be full of color, yet there would be a trace of wistfulness here and there, and a hint of something elfish, combined with all its brilliancy.

TO STUDY THE POLONAISE

Play slowly and firmly at first, each hand alone; study the phrases in detail. I find the most successful fingering for the little group of small notes in right hand, preceding the first measure, is 123-12345, as is generally given. Hold the melody notes—the quarters, dotted quarters and so on, while playing the accompaniments lightly and crisply. The group of sixteenths beginning fourth measure, should be fingered 21245 in right hand. The piece starts with mezzo tone power, diminishes to piano, then gradually increases in tone from third to ninth measure, where the tone reaches fortissimo, with vehemently marked accents. After passing the descending octave figures, we have a quieter passage as before, with an oncoming crescendo which culminates in an ascending of splendid octaves, after which come five sonorous chords. These can be graded dynamically thus:

FF, F, M, P, PP. They are directed to be played without ritard, but a slight holding back is much more effective.

The five chords introduce us to a new section marked "with passion." In this portion of the piece study everything in detail; play with firm, decisive fingers, with relaxed arm weight for chords and octaves, first with hands alone and then together; afterward study shading and effect.

In this portion we have melody in right hand, with rhythmic accompaniment, supported in second and fourth measures by a chromatic passage, swelling in the middle, like a sudden gust of wind— or passion. At the fifth measure, bring out the theme with firmness and vigor, with pedal on every beat. At top of next page we find the melody transferred to the left hand, with accompanying trills in the right hand. Make the theme prominent through resonant touch and rhythmic accents. The same theme now appears in octaves, to be played *appassionato*. The strokes are broader, the colors richer than when the passage first began. These passages of "quasi trills" should be performed by turning the hand and arm from side to side, with firm fingers, and not by employing finger action.

A big *crescendo* is now worked up through the second trill passage, the two measures of octaves and the single trill. Then, with the ascending measure of chromatics, the whole suddenly dies down to a *pianissimo,* but always with crisp accents and variety of tone. From this subdued portion again starts a *crescendo,* which gathers sweep and momentum to the end of the fourth page, when the grand passion having spent itself, the passage gradually descends to the bass, at the same time subsiding in tone. Each measure is now a little softer than the one before it; at the same time the short chromatic runs in bass should each be played with a little *crescendo* and *diminuendo.* Arrived at the lower B, we find a double trill, taken *ppp,* a mere whisper, or a dull mutter, like far-off thunder. The trill is succeeded by a brief chromatic figure. Again a murmur of trill and another chromatic figure, always with a swelling and then falling off of tone, like the throbbing of the sea. More extended chromatic waves now follow, till we finally reach the return of the first portion of the Polonaise. But the whole page as we have briefly described it, is a study of effects in light and shade. It can be made most effective if the player possesses a command of tone values.

The final page is a repetition of the first portion of the piece. It has one new passage, however—an ascending scale, which begins *pianissimo* and reaches a *fortissimo* climax in two measures. The piece closes with the former octave passage, to be played *"molto crescendo e martellato."*

The Polonaise suggests the color of scarlet to those who are fond of contrasting tones and colors. It is a rich, glowing picture of life and activity. It stirs the blood, puts rhythm into the feet, fires the imagination and should tip the fingers with flame, though at times they must be sheathed in velvet.

NUMBER VII

WAGNER-BRASSIN, "MAGIC FIRE CHARM"

Will you kindly give me some ideas about the meaning of the "Magic Fire Charm," and how to play the piece? A. L.

One of the most enchanting portions of the score of Wagner's first opera of the Ring, "Die Walküre" (always bearing in mind that "Das Rheingold" forms the Introduction to the Trilogy), is the closing scene, where *Wotan,* after a long scene with his daughter, places her upon the rocky couch where, at his bidding, flames begin to leap and play about the spot where *Brunhilde* begins her long sleep.

The translation of an orchestral piece to the piano medium is always an uncertain undertaking; yet the piano is surely the only instrument that can reproduce the effects that have been created in the orchestra. While we cannot, on the piano, realize the *klang* of the various instruments whose interweaving have wrought such wonderful effects in the selection we shall examine, a resourceful player, who understands variety of touch, tone and artistic pedalling, can give many shades of tone quality and color, which will serve to set forth the composition in its true light and meaning. And remember that for Wagner's music the pianist needs a rich color scheme which will combine all the tonal qualities contained within our instrument—the piano.

With a clear sense that we shall be expected to produce all qualities of touch and tone—able to color the touch in every conceivable way, also the necessity of using the pedals with skill and understanding, we take up one of the most striking and original compositions written for any instrument. The musician who has translated the piece from the orchestra, so that it is made possible for the piano, is the Belgian-French pianist and composer, Louis Brassin. This musician studied with Moscheles at the Leipsiz Conservatory. Later he was one of the faculty of the Stern Conservatory, Berlin. He followed this by a number of years at the Brussels Conservatory, from '69-'78, and finally became Professor at the Petrograd Conservatory. His career was brief, as he was born at Aix-la-Chapelle in 1840 and passed away at Petrograd in 1884. His time was filled with teaching, alternating with concert tours and composing. He wrote the *Ecole Moderne du Piano,* many piano études and transcriptions, even two operas. Of the "Fire Music" he created the most faithful and successful reproduction we have; there is no other translation that can be compared with it. And he has performed a service to all pianists who wish to reproduce on their instrument this vivid color poem in tones.

The moment in the unfoldment of the musical story, namely, when the fire is called forth, is at the close of the long scene between *Wotan* and his favorite daughter. He has chided her severely for her compassion for *Sieglinde* and the assistance she gave her in time of need. As punishment for thus helping a mortal, *Brunhilde* is condemned to lie asleep on a rock, until her predestined liberator, a knight without fear, shall awaken her. The fire will protect her from the approach of any who are not worthy.

In vain has *Brunhilde* besought her father, on her knees, for a reversal of this harsh sentence; she has humbled herself to the dust, in one of the most poignant appeals ever composed. But *Wotan* is deaf to all entreaties, though his anger is past. He tenderly embraces the maiden, as he leads her to the fateful couch. Already overcome by stupor she unresistingly allows herself to be placed upon it, her hands crossed upon her breast, the shield, her badge of office as one of the *Walkure* maidens, placed over them, the helmet adjusted above her fair curls. When these preparations have been completed, *Wotan* bends over her in sad contemplation and presses a farewell kiss upon her upturned face. Now he lifts himself as from a dream and waves his spear. Then the *Wotan* theme, those fateful descending octaves, resounds in the orchestra.

Let us now open the piano piece and see how the music expresses the picture.

For the first two pages we have the "Slumber Motive" expressed in chords, accompanied by those rolling arpeggios, like great waves from the sea of tone. Analyze these chords and you will find that almost every measure represents a different tonality. For this reason there is no key signature. First play the succession of chords alone, with rich, warm tone, controlled by relaxed arm weight. The theme starts with an A flat chord; then follow B, B flat and a transition into E, E flat and so on. When the chords are well in hand, and memorized if possible, turn your attention to the arpeggios. Practice them each hand alone, with firm touch, slant- ing hand and arm, that is to say, in arpeggio rela- tion of hands to the keys, the thumb deftly passing under the right hand, as it executes the backward movement. With this preparation the two parts can now be put together, taking care that the theme stands out and the accompanying arpeggios are smooth, flowing but subdued. An added refinement of interpretation—in fact a little artistic trick—is to take each chord, when written in whole notes, silently, *after* the arpeggio has been played; the pedal is of course held, and the effect thus obtained is one of ethereal tonal beauty.

Upon the serene calm of this ideal dream breaks the "Fire Motive," with all its lurid charm. On the stage flames begin to send up their tongues of light from most unexpected angles, until they make a circle of fire around the couch of the sleeping maiden. The key is the cheerful brilliant E major. Here it is imperative for the player to study the music, hands separately, for nothing can be accomplished with effects until the technical side is thoroughly mastered. Touch and tone must be brilliant, sparkling. The tones should fairly crackle; they must be played *staccatissimo,* as directed, and tossed off with the greatest sureness and ease. The chords, except those in dotted or half notes, are to be executed with extreme staccato, using an up-movement, and springing up off the keys with clenched fingers. Those who have followed and profited by the Self-Help Lessons in technic, will readily understand the necessary movements; others are advised to study into the subject of staccato chords before attempting these effects in pieces.

We have now considered the first three lines of the "Fire Theme," up to the change of key. After preparing each hand separately, study hands together, beginning softly and gradually increasing in strength. At the fourth measure *mezzo forte* is reached, and at the change of key, *forte.* In two measures more we have a *fortissimo,* and still the power and force increase. These two *ff* measures are perhaps the most troublesome in the piece. Not much can be done with them until first mastered mentally. The climax of the page is found at the last line, at the *fff* entrance. These arpeggiated chords in bass are rolled with the greatest power and abandon, closing the hand after each chord.

Dr. William Mason, in playing the piece, made a wonderful effect here, in power and volume of tone.

The crests of the waves have gathered force and momentum to the climax; they now subside very gradually, with each chord, till all die away in a shadowy *pianissimo*.

The next division is to be taken at a very moderate tempo. Through the rich tonal fabric of orchestral color, we find interwoven three themes. First the "Slumber Motive," with its caressing tenderness—dream compelling. Then the two notes in each measure given to the left hand, which crosses over the right to play them. They suggest the "Fire Theme," and must be very staccato. Finally, at the fourth measure, the "Siegfried Theme" enters. In the orchestra it is intoned in splendid brass. What a master was Wagner, to handle each theme individually and yet fuse them all into such consummate unity of effect.

In working out this complex fabric, the pianist has his hands literally full. Let a word be said for each part. The accompaniment, of continuous broken chord figures, must be skilfully managed. It must have perspective, be very smooth and even, no one note sticking out inadvertently to mar the idea of unobtrusive support. Accompanying parts are apt to be too prominent or slighted; they are either too loud or too soft. Their office is to support the melody with distinction. For no note in a piece of good music is unimportant. In the present instance practice the figures until they are clear and even; see that the fourth finger does its work and plays with the same quality of tone used by the other fingers. To bring out the "Slumber Motive," press down on the thumb with arm weight. This is simple when the melody note stands by itself; when it is joined to the octave above the task is a bit more strenuous. When the fourth measure is reached, play the "Siegfried Theme" in bass alone first, then join it with the chord. In this case the theme-note and the chord are played with firm, ringing tone; then the other tones are at once released and the single tone of the theme resounds alone. This is the only way to bring out the desired effect of this ringing theme in bass.

And finally, note well the two left hand staccato notes, which hover over each measure, and suggest little tongues of flame, as they dart upward. They must glow and glitter like brilliant points of light —like crystals shining in the sun.

The pronouncement of the "Siegfried Theme," which dominates the picture, occupies about eight measures, which have been gradually increasing in tone, until the ff is reached. At this point the whole structure gathers power and volume. The "Siegfried Theme" now resounds in octaves and big chords; the "Fire Theme" is more complete, and of course, always staccato; the "Slumber Motive" mingles with the ensemble and all reach a triumphant climax at top of page seven.

From here on tone and power gradually diminish and fall off. It is as if twilight were beginning to settle down upon the fair dreamer. The more meditative portion of the "Siegfried Theme" is heard; the "Slumber Motive" continues, and the little points of light and fire are there, but as though seen and heard through a dim and vaporous atmosphere.

At bottom of the eighth page two or three full chords again arrest attention; but on the whole the dream magic gains more and more potency; the last page is occupied with a long *diminuendo* and *ritardando,* as the harmonies mount upward, until they end in a final ascending arpeggio, and seem to melt into the invisible beyond.

This composition is one of the most thrilling of the Wagner transcriptions, and well worth the pianist's study, since there are so many varieties of touch, pedaling, tone color and theme-development to be found in it.

NUMBER VIII

CHOPIN-LISZT, "THE MAIDEN'S WISH"

"If you would give some idea of the meaning of the Chopin-Liszt *Maiden's Wish* and how it should be played, it would greatly aid a young player."

T. M.

A set of six Polish songs, composed by Chopin, has been transcribed for the piano. The Polish composer surely did not originate these melodies, for they are evidently the folk songs of the people. One is called *Springtime*, and seems to express, or rather endeavors to voice in some way the longing and expectancy of Nature for the new life that is coming.

Another tells of a young girl who receives a ring given her by her lover, and of her shy hopes and joys. The fourth is a gay *Bacchanale*, where, with *glissando* runs and explosive accents, is pictured a scene of mad merry making. And yet, in the midst of the wildest frolic, a sad, sweet strain, found in *Das Ringlein*, the young girl and her ring, which preceded it—peeps out.

Number five is called *My Joys*, and is a favorite song with Polish singers. The theme is one of tender longing. Liszt has made of it a beautiful

Nocturne; the tender theme being interspersed with elaborate cadenzas and *fioriture*. The sixth is called *The Homecoming,* and is short and gay.

These accompanying pieces of the set have been mentioned for the reason they should be better known. Indeed it is safe to say that many who play *Maiden's Wish,* have never heard of the companion numbers, which they would surely enjoy playing. Liszt's Six Transcriptions are dedicated to the Princess Sayn-Witgenstein, a lady to whom he seemed much attached, and who is said to have greatly influenced his later years.

The Maiden's Wish, the first number of the set, opens with a little figure which prefixes a small cadenza, that soars up and back again. This passage must be well managed, must have *crescendo* and *diminuendo,* and of course an *accellerando,* and should be very smooth and even. Be sure and lift the hand when the E is reached, and make a decided break before starting on the first figure again. In the opening figure, the two grace notes should be played with second and fourth fingers, with third finger on principal note.

The opening figure—now consisting of three measures—occurs four times, and must be varied each time, in quality and dynamics, to avoid monotony. For instance: the first time it is played *mezzo forte,* as though it were in the sunlight; the answer, an octave higher, will be in the shadow and played softer. Again the theme, this time louder, and its repetition softer than before, and dying away.

In place of the two grace notes in the theme, we now have a trill marked for the first beat of the measure. This can be treated in the same way as before—that is, with two grace notes, or with a small trill. Von Bülow advised the use of four trill notes, which, with the principal, made five. This, however, is a point that may be left to the skill and taste of the player.

The song proper starts at the *Meno Allegro,* at top of second page. A sweetly-moving melody, to be played expressively but not sentimentally. Play at first without pedal, allowing the tones to sound with their own beauty. Be sure and lift the hand and separate the two eighths from the second beat, in the measures where they occur. After eight measures the second half of theme appears in bass, finishing with a tiny cadenza. Use soft pedal for this, and separate the B from the A at return of first half of theme. It is suggested to repeat the second half of theme—the whole passage up to *Tempo primo.* Play Tempo One a little brighter, and at the higher repetition quite softly.

Variant I. Here we have the theme, but with many little subtle, graceful changes. It seems to be looking out at us from behind a veil. This always brings to mind an art work once seen abroad. In one of the European sculpture galleries stands a beautiful marble statue. It represents the figure of a young girl standing on tiptoe, her arms crossed lightly over her breast. Over face and figure is thrown a thin gossamer veil, through which every detail of the girl's lovely features and pliant body is seen. The vision of that marble comes to mind in studying these variations, where the theme seems to be playing hide-and-seek before our eyes.

In this first Variation, phrase the right hand very carefully according to the marks, and see that accents mark the third beat of each measure, also that the left hand uses rotary arm weight movements for chords.

Do not play the small cadenza too fast, but comfortably and elegantly. At the close, lift the hand at the A, and slightly accent the G, as it precedes a repetition of the Variant. The usual interlude follows, which starts briskly and *rinforzando,* but dies away slowly and softly.

Variant II. Practice this portion hands alone, until the right hand can execute the triplets smoothly and fluently, without a hitch. Bring out slightly the dotted half note in left hand, as it forms a sort of foundation to the whole. After the double bar, play left hand chords lightly and *staccato.* The first page merges into an extended passage which should start *mezzo forte,* increase, then become softer, down to *pianissimo.* The second page should have the left hand pairs accented on first of each pair, while triplets in right have the first note of each slightly emphasized all through.

Variant III. Brings us to the climax. Starting softly, there are strong, rhythmic accents on each octave in right hand, and on quarter and half notes in left. Repeat the two lines before proceeding. Tempo and power now increase, until, at the seventh measure from the repeat, "everything can be thrown out of the window," as Liszt himself might have said, and the next six or seven measures are loud and fast. A slight ritard occurs at the end of the chord passage, and a pause ensues before the *Vivace* begins.

Begin the *Vivace* with a crisp brightness and with well-marked accents. Play *forte* for four measures. The following four measures are piano, with a gradual falling off in tone from here to the end. Use soft pedal for second half of page, and let all die away in a soft, delicate murmur. These delicate effects are more difficult to manage than the loud portions. In practice use firm, clear touch, with well-articulated finger action. Occasionally play rapidly and softly, with fingers held close to the keys; then return to slow tempo and firm touch. Only in this way can a clear, beautiful *pianissimo* be acquired, which will not sound fuzzy and impure.

PART THREE

In our quest for well-arranged programmes and their artistic interpretation, we should be able to gain inspiration from considering those performed by the master pianists of our time.

In any of our great music centers one may see and hear in constant succession these master spirits; may weigh, balance and compare the work of each in various demonstrations of their prowess. Sometimes they elect to play solely the music of old composers, or only that of the moderns. Often they arrange an eclectic list which progresses through the various epochs from classic down to the present moment. Sometimes they choose the music of one composer, and one programme as placed on record, where all the music was written in a single key. Naturally the big compositions for the piano are performed a number of times each season, by different artists. This gives the serious student of the piano a wonderful opportunity to contrast the various readings.

It is acknowledged that each artist if he is really a master, plays in an individual way. He has his own little shadings, tempos, nuances and so on. In fact he expresses himself through the music he plays. This individuality does not actually change the general scheme of interpretation, but renders his reading distinctive. If the young pianist can capture some of the ideas thus suggested, they give him a vision of what may be accomplished by the genius of the artist. Not that he should slavishly copy such details—though rather imitate than play in a wooden, uninteresting manner—but that he should thus gain ideas of style, so important a factor in forming the well-equipped player.

Though pointing out the salient ideas found in the artist's rendering of a fine work, it is not the intention here to criticize his conception; that must be left to the professional critics. Nor will it be said that we prefer more poetry in this place, less pounding in the other; more dwelling on beautiful details here, more virility there.

The way to study style and interpretation, to learn all we can of each, is to take only the greatest master players, the super-pianists, as models. And this is what we have endeavored to do in the following studies. These studies, though brief, are the result of repeated hearings, much thoughtful consideration of the compositions performed and often talks with the artists themselves about their work.

AN AFTERNOON WITH RACHMANINOFF

Medtner, *Improvisation;* Weber, *Rondo Brilliante;* Chopin, *Polonaise, Nocturne, Valse, Sonata, Op. 35;* Moszkowski, *Juggleress;* Liszt, *Etude, D flat;* Strauss, *Blue Danube.*

The name of Sergei Rachmaninoff is known all over the world, wherever music itself is known. After successes in many parts of the globe, he came and conquered America, as he had other lands. He must have liked it in this country so well that he returned to remain here. He is now one of us; his music and his playing are becoming more and more familiar. Students and music lovers flock to his recitals, which are often sold out long in advance.

With all this popularity, there surely cannot be many music lovers who have not heard the distinguished Russian in recital. If there be a pianist to whom circumstances has denied that pleasure, let him come with me, and we will listen mentally to a typical programme, such as was given not long ago, in the largest concert hall of the metropolis.

Do not imagine that this tall, austere-looking personality, who walks with stately step across the stage and seats himself solemnly before the instrument, is in reality as forbidding as he looks, or that he will play as severely as his manner would indicate. On the contrary, you will find him capable of expressing every shade of emotion that he desires to depict, be it sad or gay; while if you should approach him back stage, he would greet you with kind seriousness.

His large, expressive hands are able to reach widespread chords without "breaking" them; his tone is very musical, and never harsh, even in the loudest passages. He has great velocity, power, delicacy, in short every quality but perhaps deeply felt tenderness—something not one in a thousand can express at the piano. In every other way you will realize, after he has played a quarter of an hour, that he has complete control of his instrument and of himself, and that his playing is masterly in the highest degree. Watch his hands as they leave the keys. Do you ever see them thrown back from the wrist? No; the wrist draws them up; the wrist leads.

He sits quietly before the instrument for a moment or so, as if lost in thought. Then, without a note of prelude, he begins an *Improvisation,* by a modern Russian—Medtner. It is by way of introduction, and leads to—what? Even Weber's *Rondo Brilliante.* The young pianist of today, who revels in Debussy and Stravinsky, disdains to play Weber; he is too obvious and old-fashioned. But the great Russian pianist-composer does not disdain this music. With what devotion he plays it; what crisp delicacy and clarity are here, what refinement of phrasing and variety of tone. And withal there is such buoyant gaiety through every measure. It is indeed a lesson to young players to find such old but ever youthful compositions interpreted by a master, as they should be, without affectation or exaggeration.

Next comes some Chopin—a *Polonaise, Nocturne, Valse,* followed by the *Sonata Op. 35.* Like Paderewski, Rachmaninoff does not indicate on the programme the key and Opus number of the Chopin pieces; he chooses at will and according to mood.

The Polonaise proved to be Op. 26, in C sharp minor, so seldom heard, yet so beautiful when imbued with the right spirit. This time it was set forth in the "grand manner." The sweep of the opening chords—crisp and powerful—was followed by the capricious passages which were pregnant with meaning.

After the double bar, one noticed that the ascending runs, between the chords, were *ripped off,* as it were, by drawing the hands from the top keys, at the same time closing the fingers quickly, which gave a very brilliant effect.

The D flat portion was expressive, though reposeful. The dynamics and shadings seemed infinite, and gave the impression of an improvisation. Instead of closing as players generally do, the pianist

turned back to the beginning and repeated the first
portion. The idea was effective, and is really what
the composer has indicated.

The Nocturne chosen was in F sharp, Op. 15,
No. 2, one that all young girls play (they could
learn how to do it from such a lucid interpretation
as this!). No doubt the middle section, with its
"Doppio movimento" has puzzled many young
pianists, as to why Chopin seemed to change the
rhythm right in the middle. They may be com-
forted to know that Rachmaninoff made no appre-
ciable difference between the rhythms; both sounded
the same as he played them.

The *Valse in F major, Op. 34, No. 3* is also
heard more frequently in the studio than on the
concert platform. All was rapid, fluent, with much
variety of light and shade. The passage with grace
notes in right hand, was taken *forte,* with very
crisp touch; the spirit of the whole was cheerful
and buoyant; none of the *morbidezza* which so
many amateurs put into everything they touch of
Chopin.

All of the foregoing had but led, step by step,
to the peak of the programme, the Chopin *Sonata
in B flat minor.* Schumann says that Chopin bound
together four of his maddest children in this Sonata. As our pianist unfolded the first movement,
his fingers seemed tipped with fire; the phrases
seemed to glow and burn with the intensity of emotion, with variety of feeling. Then came the

Scherzo, that unapproachable, flashing, triumphant thing, which so few players can project with the passion it suggests. Rachmaninoff could do it. His upward figures of double fourths and sixths had the big crescendos that are needed, and then the crashing chords, which reach such a climax of passion, began to die down, to meet the lovely *Trio in G flat,* that "song of songs," as it has been called. Here it is indeed a "flower between two abysses," for the first portion of the *Scherzo* returns, played more vehemently than before. How exciting it was, the power and sweep which the artist put into it.

And after it the *Funeral March.* Every school girl agonizes over this; it has become so familiar that it appeals even to the popular taste, especially the song-like middle portion. The composer's idea seemed to be a solemn march by a military band. It is first heard in the distance, very softly. The tone increases as the funeral cortège approaches until full power is reached with those great chordal masses of sound. Then a sudden hush falls and the celestial melody of the middle section is intoned. It is grief stricken, yet strives to give consolation. It leaves the earth clods behind and lifts thought to the contemplation of higher things, to the realm of spirit. How few pianists can express this exaltation of thought and feeling! Paderewski can; Gabrilowitsch very nearly; both take it slowly, for it is never impressive when played fast, even in small degree. One must have every shade of tonal color on the palette, and put them at the service of spiritual thought, in order to convey the message of the music.

Returning to the original theme, Rachmaninoff takes it up *fortissimo,* and gradually diminishes in tone to the end. This is logical, if the band takes up its burden of song, and passes slowly away to the distance. But most of the pianists begin softly, working up a gradual *crescendo,* then diminishing until *pianissimo* is reached.

The *Presto* is wonderful, as it is bound to be in the hands of a great artist. "Night winds sweeping over graves in the churchyard," it has been named. It seems uncanny, unearthly, with its unquiet figures, that rush up and down the keyboard as if searching for something they cannot find. Withal a remarkable ending to a superlative work. Rachmaninoff gave it just the spirit of unrest, of mysterious ghostliness it seems to embody.

The tension was now relieved by some lighter music. Two charming bits by the master himself, a *Melodie* and *Serenade.* So far as notes go, these are accessible to young pianists, and are delightful to play. The composer gave them both quite simply, with delicate sentiment.

Moszkowski's *Juggleress* seemed very appropriate just here. It was tossed off with crisp, delicate staccato touch, in the spirit of railery and humor. This is an excellent medium to cultivate the light staccato, or the slapping touches, both of which may be used.

The ever beautiful *Etude in D flat,* of Liszt, was
the vehicle for much lovely tone color, shading,
variety of power, delicacy and accent. The passages seemed to float in ether as they ascended,
while the melody sang above all the surrounding
lacework of accompaniment.

The *"Blue Danube,"* of Strauss-Schultz-Evler,
closed the printed programme. Needless to say it
was given with all the consummate control and
wealth of technical resource of which Rachmaninoff
is capable.

After it was over the master added seven or eight
other pieces to his list, many of them short salon
pieces of his own, or his countrymen. Among them
were *The Maiden's Wish,* of Chopin-Liszt, the little
Valse, Op. 40, by Tschaikowsky, which the artist
always plays so charmingly, and which is highly
recommended to young players.

As a finale, his own always demanded *Prelude
in C sharp minor,* was added, played as he wants it
to be played! No Rachmaninoff audience will ever
leave the hall until it has listened to this threadbare,
yet always impressive composition, and the composer always yields to the demand.

JOSEF HOFMANN IN A SCHUMANN PROGRAMME

Schumann *Symphonic Variations, Op. 13; Des Abends, In der Nacht, Bird as Prophet, Contrabandista, Romance in F sharp, Carneval, Op. 9.*

"Hofmann and Schumann in conjunction," I said, looking at the programme for the first time, as I settled in my seat in a receptive and expectant mood. The Polish pianist had been winning golden opinions in other parts of the world and had returned covered with honors. It was said of him that his art had ripened and mellowed, until it was the quintessence of all that was beautiful and perfect.

The programme contained but three groups. Beginning with the *Symphonic Variations,* and including a few short pieces, it closed with the *Carneval, Op. 9,* that fascinating kaleidoscope of moods and tenses of the heart. Just these, but within these somewhat narrow boundaries, what may not a great artist like Hofmann create?

And now those simple, noble harmonies of the Theme for the Variations are heard. What tone, what quality! What variety, delicacy, power! The notes are all there, in just the right balance and relation to each other, neither more nor less tone than is required. All the fine points in artistic play-craft are noted; here a special accent, there another; here a bit of theme standing out, and being answered by other voices in succession. How sane and simple it all sounds, just as we, in our best moments, would wish it to sound. There is nothing to grate on the ear; every tone has its just amount of force, its allotted place in the musical pattern.

"That is the most beautiful Steinway I have ever heard," said a lady at my elbow. "I saw it at the factory. It was specially made for the artist. There is a large amount of extra work on it. The keyboard is so smoothed and polished that there is never a suggestion of flaw or roughness anywhere. Even the sides of the keys are ivory-covered."

As each Variation unrolls before us, we marvel at the clearness and meaning with which it is set forth, the infinite gradations of tone in tint and nuance. Ah, here is the last Variation before the March. He takes it slowly, tenderly, in subdued half-lights; thus played it makes a moving appeal. The two voices in right hand hold exquisite converse, while the left hand murmurs an accompaniment. How can other players rush it through as they so often do; how can they have the heart?

As those wonderful tones fade into silence, there comes a long pause. Hofmann knows the artistic value of the pause, just as Paderewski does. One can scarcely breathe; the many seconds of stillness seem so many moments charged with poignant emotion.

Now comes the March, clear, vigorous, with ringing accents, thunderous crescendos and great dynamic variety. Here arms come into full play; arm weight is paramount. Sometimes, when the music requires, arms are lifted together with the greatest precision, and fall on the keyboard with absolute accuracy of movement, proving that accuracy never interferes with artistic interpretation. On the contrary it is the backbone of all that is best in piano mechanism.

Five shorter pieces follow the stupendous Variations: they are polished gems of purest ray. First comes "Evening," of the *Fantasie Stucke, Op. 12.* How tenderly the theme is played in the upper voice, as little phrases in other voices answer. All is smooth and polished in every detail.

"But you know Hofmann has a wonderful hand for the piano, perfect from every point of view," said my neighbor.

With a perfect hand and an ideal instrument, miracles may be accomplished *if* the mind of the artist, the moving power of all, be attuned to the highest ideals.

"In the Night," follows "Evening." This is almost uncanny in its swiftness. Demons seem to be abroad; accents are sharp, like flashes of lightning; the sky is lurid with thunder clouds. Hofmann's conception of this passionate mood has always been graphic. Now, in his mature mastery of style, the colors have perceptibly deepened, and the whole becomes more impressive.

The beautiful F sharp major Romance brings relief from the gloomy terrors of the night. Here all is serene tenderness and gentleness, such as the artist, who can well be compared to his famous compatriot, Paderewski, knows so well how to impart. In this Romance tone quality, together with balance of parts, are of prime importance. The hand of a master can paint the picture in just the exact tints.

And now the picture is lightened yet more through the *Prophet Bird,* that soars skyward with the most ethereal tones imaginable. Nothing could be more delicate than those little up-turning runs— so smooth, so filmy-light—like fleecy clouds. No heavy hand can be used here; all must be of exceeding delicacy. The middle section is a tender song, sung by the top notes of the chords; it ritards at the close and melts into the return of the first part of the piece.

At the close of this group came the Tausig transcription of Schumann's song, *The Contrabandista,* a brilliant morceau, especially suited to Hofmann's pellucid technic and limpid tone quality. He plays it with great rapidity; accents are like points of light. He never loses sight of the theme, no matter how much it is overshadowed by surrounding embroideries. The listeners are enthused and the piece must be repeated.

The *Carneval*, a collection of short pieces, depicts, in a sense, the merriment of a masquerade. Some of the pieces are named from characters in the masked ball, such as *Pierrot, Harlequin, Columbine* and *Pantaloon*, while others represent real friends. Among them we meet members of the *Davidsbund* —*Florestan, Eusebius, Chiarina* (Clara), Ernestine von Fricken (*Estrella*), *Chopin* and *Paganini*. There is also a *Coquette*, but it is not known for whom this was intended. Besides these some of the pieces are named from occurrences at the ball, such as *Recognition*, an *Avowal of Love*, a *Promenade*, and so on. He has called them *Reconnaissance, Aveu, Promenade*, and *Pause*. The *Papillon* theme peeps out once or twice. The Finale is called *March of the Davidsbundler against the Philistines*. Here is found the Grandfather's Dance, a tune of the 17th century. It has been said that Schumann felt he had to put a poetical or descriptive title to a piece, since the notes alone might not say all he wanted to express.

The pianist interpreted these poetic pieces with consummate mastery. Every great artist plays them but few seem to fathom their true meaning, or have the equipment to reveal this nosegay of blossoms to us in all their fragrance and beauty. A player must possess a highly-trained imagination to get into the skin of these various moods. It seemed the pianist on this occasion revealed the inherent imagination, fancy, humor and poetry, with greater perfection than ever before. He showed a constant play of the qualities which Schumann has so richly embodied in his music.

Such interpretations are illuminating to piano student and teacher. While the mastery is the fine flower of all the qualities of mind and heart, it has its roots in a splendid technical foundation of perfect preparation.

First of all there is clearness of enunciation. All great pianists play distinctly, just as the greatest actors have good diction. This means carefully cultivated finger action, always kept in repair. Next is the wonderful feeling for rhythm, which never loses time or beat. Hofmann has this gift of rhythm, yet he has a metronome on the piano in his work room, and advocates its use. If he, so gifted, does so, what of lesser men, of students and young players? Shall they complain of the troublesome metronome, which shows them their faults, and aids in correcting them? One might as well complain of troublesome truth.

Third, dynamics. This is a wide subject, almost unexplored by the young student. How seldom he thinks about shading scales, arpeggios, chords or trills. It is fascinating study. After listening to the purling or thunderous scales of Hofmann, let us go home and try to imitate them. Also let us try to imitate the imagination with which such an artist invests the smallest piece, illumines the smallest phrase. Pursue this path and it will lead us higher and higher.

III

Liszt, *Sonata, B minor;* Schumann, *Etudes Symphoniques;* Chopin, *Twenty-Four Preludes.*

We have just considered the value and meaning of a programme interpreted by Josef Hofmann, which was a model of simplicity and beauty.

Following the appearance of the Polish pianist, another programme was heard in this same Carnegie Hall, offered by the distinguished French pianist, Alfred Cortot. This programme was built on broad, romantic lines and contained three works only, the Liszt *B minor Sonata,* Schumann's *Symphonic Variations* and Chopin's *Twenty-Four Preludes.* Here was food for dreams, for passion, exhaltation and every uplifting thought and emotion. Where in the whole realm of piano literature, for instance, is there a work more vital, more alive with poignant emotion than is Liszt's noble Sonata? To the sympathetic student of his works, this Sonata stands out as expressing his inner experiences. Its meaning is so intimate, yet so broad and sweeping, so tremendous in weight of expressiveness, that no player save a great artist should ever attempt the work in public. None but a master, with mental, physical and emotional equipment able to portray this vision of the inner life of the composer, ought to lay hands on such a unique epic.

In his exposition of it Cortot proved himself such a master. His performance was electrifying. The French artist commands a technic equal to every demand. It is true other pianists nowadays possess colossal technic. But what of the ability to play notes merely, when the interpretation of such a work is considered? It is the quality of the tone Cortot produces that grips, from first to last. It is the intensity of each note, chord and phrase, which carries the message. Every note seemed to glow and burn, sometimes with a soft lambent flame, as in the chant; again with the rush of a fiery tornado. Yet in the most powerful passages there was never a harsh, brittle quality; it was deep intensity without sharpness or bitterness. Such a performance is always an inspiration, and proves there is much more to piano playing than depressing correct keys.

The Liszt Sonata, with its burning fervor and lofty sweep, was perhaps too exalted for some of the listeners. They might even have found the *Symphonic Variations,* played with marvelous interpretative skill, a little too high in the clouds. But the Chopin Preludes came nearer the heart and spoke to everyone, often in the simplest language. It is of these and their interpretation that we would especially speak at present, although we have already referred to a few of the Preludes in earlier programmes.

The French pianist seems to play these gems of piano music with peculiar affection and understanding, and they are an especially sympathetic medium for his refined art. He seems to have fathomed all the emotions they depict, as though they were peculiarly his own. He has set down in words his idea of the meaning of each little piece, and says that, though it may seem presumptuous to add a single remark to the musical thought, he does not feel he is overstepping the mark in acting the modest role of interpreter, or in aiding the listener to evoke with him, the romantic figures, ardent, poetic or desperate, that suggest themselves to him in this, the most wonderful music of history.

Let us follow his inspiring suggestions as we listen to his playing.

Prelude 1, "Waiting feverishly for the beloved." Cortot accents the *lower* line of melody notes, those produced with thumb of right hand, not the upper line. Artists differ in conception of this Prelude; Gabrilowitsch and Hofmann mingle the two styles.

With No. 2 we seem plunged in the deepest woe; it is sorrow unrelieved by a single ray of light. No wonder the artist calls it "Sad meditations; in the distance a deserted sea." He puts this feeling into his playing and we feel it with him.

It is a relief to come upon No. 3, the "Song of the Brook." Here the left hand ripples up and down in delicate *leggiero,* ebbing and flowing in many nuances. The right hand melody is quite free in movement of arm, and sings itself over the undulating bass.

Again we are in the depths of woe in No. 4, which he calls "Beside a Tomb." This was exquisitely played, the chords in left hand forming one continuous undertone of subdued harmony—the upper theme suffused with emotion. Two points were noted: the grace note in measures 11 and 19 was played as an eighth note, and the three chords at close were released—not held—their time.

"A Tree Full of Song," well describes No. 5, which seems vocal with many bird notes.

"Homesickness," is the thought of No. 6. The artist brought out the bass theme all through, playing the right hand softly, as a background and slightly breaking the double notes. At the 7th and 8th measures the right hand sings above the bass. The last line is well-nigh inaudible it is so shadowy. De Pachmann also rendered it in this way.

No. 7 is a tiny Mazurka, in which "delicious recollections float like perfume through the memory." It was sweet but fleeting and there was no repetition of its sixteen measures, as Paderewski often gave.

No. 8 was fascinating in its ebb and flow of melody. To the listener it suggested gaiety and brightness, but for the pianist "the snow falls, the wind howls, the tempest rages, but in my sad heart

there is a more terrible storm." The storm calmed
at the close and the final chords were not "broken."

"The End of Poland" is the motto of the 9th
Prelude. It was played broadly and intensely. At
the start the accompaniment was most subdued;
the theme also was moderate in tone. Gradually
this broad, simple theme gained in strength and momentum, until it closed in a climax of power and
sonority.

No. 10 is called "Falling Rockets." It is played
lightly, with fairy-like deftness and swiftness. The
bass is also given out softly. At such a tempo, it is
almost over before one is aware. The listeners
hoped it would be repeated, but in vain.

"A Young Girl's Wish," is the sweet, alluring
title for the 11th Prelude. It, too, was played
softly, with lovely tone quality, the undulating figures rising and falling like the breath of innocence
and youth.

No. 12, in G sharp minor, was taken at a terrific
tempo, yet all was clear and well articulated. The
artist calls it "The Rider in the Night." One must
recall Schumann's "In the Night." Both suggest
the uncanny, the awesome. After working up a big
crescendo on the second page, the passion subsides
little by little, until the player ends quite softly, in
spite of the marked *ff* at the close.

No. 13, Lento. "In a Strange Land, under a
starry sky, thinking of the loved one far away."
In expressing this mood the player began very

softly, using much soft pedal throughout.   The left
hand especially was subdued.   The *piu lento* section
sang with slightly more prominence, but at the return of *Tempo* I the bass once more becomes a
murmur, ending in a deeper shadow.

No. 14, "A Stormy Sea."   In this Cortot creates
a big crescendo, working it up from the beginning
to the middle, where it reaches a *ff*, then subsides to
an almost inaudible murmur at the close.

No. 15.   So much has been written about the D
flat Prelude that little more can be said.   We have
heard of "rain dropping from the eaves," of
"knights in armor," of the composer's gruesome
fancies when left alone at night in an old castle.
Cortot conceives this Prelude as a tender cradle
song, a vision of a young mother rocking her baby
to sleep.   Tender and appealing in the first section,
throbbing with feeling in the middle portion, soft
and shadowy on the return of first theme.   Like de
Pachmann, Cortot ended with almost inaudible
tone; all seemed to fade into silence.

No. 16, "The Road to the Abyss."   Naturally this
was taken at a whirlwind speed, but with remark-
ably controlled shadings, which prevented any
monotony, and with plenty of accent.   The whole
glowed with life and color, like a brilliant jewel.
The final chords were sharply abrupt, which gave
a fitting ending, and awoke the listener as from
a trance.

No. 17.   Perhaps the noblest of them all, this has

had many interpretations. To Cortot it is evidently a love song, for his motto is "She told me she loved me." Tender and ardent was his playing of it. At the entrance of these "booming A flats," to quote Huneker, which Paderewski intoned with such deep, mysterious power, Cortot played them much softer than many pianists, not more than *mezzo forte,* with a gradual *diminuendo* to the close.

No. 18. The term for this is "Imprecations," and it was delivered with fiery passion, strong accents and breathless speed. Heavy accents were placed on chords of sixth measure from end, while both closing chords were released abruptly, thereby heightening the effect.

No. 19 was exquisite, the effect of soaring melody preserved throughout. This effect was produced by accenting the first note of each triplet in right hand. "Had I wings I would fly to you, my beloved," is the motto, and the piece was played *con amore.* Final chord soft.

No. 20 he calls "Funerals." The stately chords, so sonorous and powerful at first, gradually recede into the dim distance, like a passing funeral cortège. At fourth beat of third measure, the pianist played E natural instead of E flat, which some other players use.

The nocturne-like Prelude No. 21, was played with beautiful variety of tone. In second measure the grace note was made long, while later on the chord of small notes corresponded with the principal chord. The closing measures where the bass passage ascends, a *diminuendo* effect was produced, instead of *crescendo*. Its motto is "Returning solitary to the spot where vows were made."

No. 22, "Revolution," was played with the spirit of the motto, with booming of guns, explosive accents and thundering octaves. The four final chords resounded like cannon.

In delicious contrast was the lovely Prelude No. 23, "Naiads at Play." Undulating passages were smooth as oil, the theme in bass with the passing trills was gracious and insinuating. The close was a diminuendo of exquisite fineness, ending almost imperceptibly.

And now came Prelude No. 24, of which great artists make a veritable *tour de force*. The motto, *"Sang de la Volupte de la Mort,"* suggests one explanation of the unrest, the passion, sweep, the whirlwind of emotion which carry the breathless listener onward from start to finish. It was brilliant piano playing, but it was more: it was life, intense, thrilling, tragic!

IV

Rachmaninoff, *Prelude;* Beethoven, *Sonata, Op. 27, No. 2;* Schumann, *Etudes Symphoniques;* Chopin, *Prelude No. 25; Nocturne, Op. 27, No. 1; Etude, Op. 10, No. 4; Etude, Op. 25, No. 7; Mazurka, Op. 41, No. 1; Fantaisie Impromptu, Op. 66; Scherzo, Op. 39;* Liszt, *Hungarian Rhapsodie, No. 12.*

In the beginning of these programme studies, it was suggested there should be variety of key as well as of material and content, when arranging the programme plan. It is a fact that artists bear this in mind when making up their lists. However, it remained for Wilhelm Bachaus to offer a programme—not of one composer but of one key. This was indeed a novelty, as it had not been done before within the writer's recollection. Mr. Bachaus proved that while he played the entire evening pieces founded in the key of C sharp minor, he had, by careful selection, arranged a programme which was far from being monotonous. Indeed it succeeded, through variety of content, in being full of interest from beginning to end.

This unique programme opened with the familiar Prelude of the Russian composer-pianist, Rachmaninoff, which the pianist gave with much of the tragic meaning the composer himself puts into it. The first page slow, the following two faster, with right hand melody well brought out, and culminating in a big climax; the final section very powerful and heroic.

In harmony with this Prelude yet of a style very different, came the so-called "Moonlight Sonata" of Beethoven. How solemn was the First Movement; it seemed all in drab, the hue of disappointment. It is said to typify the hopeless love story of the master for a woman above him in station. The Second Movement was taken lightly and simply, with no exaggeration in dynamics. The Third was played at high speed, as though under great excitement. As such it represents the rage and despair of the composer when he learned the woman he adored really belonged to another. In spite of the rapid tempo, there was always time for strong accents, shading in passages, all the little details which show perfect command over the work in hand, and the mechanism of the piano.

Close upon the Sonata followed the Schumann *Symphonic Etudes*. Bachaus gives a masterly reading of them; the projection of this great work is one of his highest achievements. Let us listen as they unroll before us.

The noble theme is quiet but sonorous.   First Variation is light with detached *leggiero* touch.

Second Variation has strong accents and expressive melody; it is played in a majestic manner.

Variation Three is lightly staccato; second half starting Forte, diminishes to an extremely soft tone.

Fourth Variation: Chords are "pulled up" with crisp touch.

Fifth Variation.   Very free wrist and arms; light touch with necessary accents.

Sixth Variation.   Those formidable left-hand skips rolled off the pianist's fingertips as though without the slightest effort—the result of long practice.   The right hand sang the theme with expressive sonority, above the restless bass.

Seventh Variation was brilliant all through, with strong accents.

The Eighth Variation seemed in the nature of an improvisation, in slow tempo, with many nuances.

Variation Nine was played, as directed, "as fast as possible."   In spite of high speed all was well articulated.   The second half had very strong accents; the final arpeggio in both hands was velvety soft, with two pedals.

Tenth Variation was played with rhythmic energy, working up a couple of big crescendos on second page.   There were strong accents on both final chords.

Variation Eleven.   With sincere feeling and true

expressiveness, this poignant music was projected. The final measures were soft and shadowy.

Then the stirring March began, the *Finale*, known as Variation 12. It was filled with vitality, with powerful highlights, many shadings, and closed with a fine climax of intensity.

A let-down from the sustained vigor of this master work came through the lovely Prelude of Chopin, Op. 28, No. 25, which the composer dedicated to Princess Czernicheff. It is not often played, not being "music for the multitude," according to Huneker, who comments on its Brahmsian coloring. It was expressively played, and its sentiment did not degenerate into mawkishness. It is so easy to overstep the mark of good taste in this direction.

Of the two Studies, the former, Op. 10, No. 4, was full of life and fire, and taken at great speed. How seldom one hears this Etude in recital. His public appreciates the Bachaus interpretation of the Chopin Etudes, for they generally insist on repetitions. At a previous recital the *Chromatic Etude, Op. 10, No. 2,* made instant appeal. It was so light, fleet and so fascinating withal, that the house rose to it, and insisted on repetition. This was granted and the piece rippled and scintillated as before. Still people were not satisfied and would not allow the programme to proceed until it had been heard for the third time.

The second Etude on the programme we are now considering was No. 7 of Op. 25, one greatly be-

loved of musicians. Von Bülow called it a nocturne
for 'cello and flute. It is indeed a lovely night song,
perhaps a love duet. The sickly and over-senti-
mental were here avoided by the pianist, who knew
how to preserve a golden mien. He sang the
melody expressively, while the scale passages were
even and flowing.

After the Etudes came one Mazurka—we could
have wished for several. The chosen one was the
first of a set of four, Op. 41. He played this lightly,
elegantly, without perhaps the variety of nuance,
of native flavor, which a Polish pianist would impart to it, but still in true musicianly style.

The *Fantaisie Impromptu, Op. 66,* was played at
a very rapid pace, as it must be. How many school
girls and young students struggle over those uneven
rhythms. Students need to be put through a
course of rhythmic scale study. First scales and
passages with two notes in one hand to three in
the other; then three notes against four. Reverse
hands and work out the same problems in the opposite direction. These exercises ought to be preliminary to the study of pieces like the *Impromptu
in C sharp minor.*

The *C sharp minor Scherzo* is for many the most
beautiful as well as the most dramatic of the four.
It is marked *Presto con fuoco,* and was begun at
whirlwind pace, up to the change of tempo to *Meno
Mosso.* Then came the noble chord theme, with
the delicate arabesque between.

No better finger practice can be suggested than these broken chord figures, for those who are keen to hunt for technical material in pieces.   Taken as a whole the projection of this Scherzo was full of virility as well as delicacy; it was built on broad lines, passionate yet always under control; delicate and forceful by turns.

Naturally the *Twelfth Rhapsodie* was a feat of brilliant display, in which the pianist employed all his art and virtuosity.   There is great technical variety in Number Twelve; many styles enter into it.   The closing portion, with its sharp dissonances, should be played quickly—as it was—in order to temper the harshness—get over it, as it were. Bachaus has the strength and endurance, the lightness as well as power, the variety of touch and tone, which can render such music with effect and conviction.   He has, too, the continuity of thought-force, that can drive through from start to finish, with no lapse of rhythmic swing or falling off in intensity.   It is great piano playing!

It must be borne in mind, that while all the pieces on this unique programme were written in the predominating Key of C sharp minor, the composers used many modulations and excursions into neighboring or remote Keys.   The compositions could not always remain in the Key of C sharp minor, though they began, and as a rule ended in this tonality.

V

A RECITAL OF PIANO MUSIC BY
OSSIP GABRILOWITSCH

Bach, *Toccata and Fugue, D;* Mozart, *Variations, in F;* Scarlatti, *Allegro, A major;* Beethoven, *Sonata, C Sharp minor, Op. 27, No. 2;* Chopin, *Impromptu, Op. 36; Valse, A flat, Op. 64; Valse, A minor, Op. 34; Valse, A flat, Op. 42;* Henselt, *"If I Were a Bird";* Paderewski, *Theme Varie, Op. 16.*

Let it be again placed on record that Mr. Gabrilowitsch is one of the great interpreters of piano music who are with us today. He uses his masterly technic, not for brilliant display but to adequately interpret the music he expresses, which he illumines by the power of an intellectual and emotional force such as only the few possess.

But we are not concerned at this moment about the many excellences of the artist's piano playing; rather will we consider the present programme, how he happened to choose these pieces, and arrange them just as he did. Also we will endeavor to gain a new light on the interpretation of the compositions themselves, that we may profit by what he can give.

184

Some players might have arranged the opening group differently, by placing the Scarlatti first, then Mozart, and the imposing *Toccata and Fugue,* by Bach, last.   However, in the working out of the scheme chosen, each piece seemed to follow in logical succession, justifying the arrangement.

The Bach was splendidly orchestral in tone, just as it should be, since it was written for organ.   The piano transcription is by Tausig, one of Liszt's favorite pupils, and has been excellently well done. The pianist gave the great work a serious and noble reading, on broad lines, yet with sympathetic touches here and there, as one feels Bach himself would have done.   One wonders if the old master would recognize his clavichord music, could he hear it now on a modern concert grand.   We can be sure that if such an instrument had been available in his day, he would have employed all its resources.

The Bach *Toccata* made a fine opening to the programme.   After the late comers had settled themselves, came the little classics, Mozart's *Variations in F,* and the Scarlatti *Allegro in A.*   Here was variety, both as to tonality and to style.   These little old pieces were unfamiliar to most of the listeners; they were in pure classic form, and were played as simply and naively as such music should be played, with unaffected sincerity.

Following these came Beethoven's *Sonata, Op. 27, No. 2,* called the *"Moonlight."*   How many stories have crept around this favorite composition; how many word pictures have tried to explain its meaning. The music should speak for itself, you say. True; but if you are to interpret it, you must have some definite idea in mind of what such a work means to you. Is it sad or gay, gloomy or bright, depressing or uplifting? If you can settle these points in your mind, you will have a basis to work from, a starting point as it were. No six artists—or even two—are going to play the "Moonlight Sonata" in exactly the same way, although each one will perform the notes as they are set down. Gabrilowitsch will not use just the same nuances that Bachaus employs, nor will Cortot's playing sound just like Hofmann's or Bauer's. The music lover can rejoice that each artist is individual, for he can thereby get various angles of vision on his favorite works.

The first movement of the Moonlight is sad, gloomy, a level of poignant despair, relieved here and there by certain tones which rise above the level by shadings, *crescendos* and *diminuendos*. It is Beethoven communing with his sad heart. The sympathetic player will contrive to impart this mood to the music. Gabrilowitsch can do this; he has a warm, sympathetic touch and tone; one can see by the expression of his face that he is entirely wrapt up in what he is doing, and oblivious of the audience.

The second movement was more cheerful, clearly

articulated and exactly phrased. In the third movement, Beethoven, it is said, expresses his despair and rage at finding the woman he adored was beyond his hopes. Some pianists take this at terrific speed, so that one is apt to lose some of the finer details. The Russian player is careful not to let this occur: all is clear, in spite of the velocity. Is it not better to reduce the speed slightly for the sake of clearness?

In his Chopin group, Gabrilowitsch was especially *en rapport* with the music. The lovely *Impromptu in F sharp* is peculiarly adapted to his style, and his playing of it was full of deep feeling. It formed a distinct contrast to the Beethoven Sonata.

This Impromptu seems much more vital than the other three. To Huneker the first section has a carillon-like bass, which recalls the faint, buried tones of Hauptmann's *Sunken Bell*. This portion should be played with swaying rhythm—*rubato,* like an improvisation. The second page, with its rhythmic bass, like hoofbeats, starting faintly, rises to a climax, and then subsides at return of first theme. Those "hoofbeats" in left hand, should *not* be played legato, but in pairs, with free arm movements. The final portion, with scale passages in right hand, should be smooth and flowing.

The *A flat Valse, Op. 64, No. 3,* Huneker calls charming, and further says of it that it is for superior souls who dance with intellectual joy, with the joy that comes of making exquisite patterns and curves. This may be all true, but there is a deeper meaning to this smaller *Valse in A flat*. At least Gabrilowitsch found it, for he made it sympathetic as well as graceful.

The *Valse in A minor* is Chopin in a despondent mood; the left hand theme makes this plain. Yet this piece was a great favorite with the composer, who preferred it to others of the set. It is slower in tempo, and should be played with true sentiment.

It was a happy idea to contrast the three Valses of different periods, keys and opus numbers. The large *Valse in A flat,* which closed the group, is considered the finest of all the eighteen. It is full of young life, pulsating movement, coquetry and charm. Its form is finished and rounded out, artistic in every line. It formed a dashing climax to the poetical, dreamy-sad Valses preceding it.

Why did Gabrilowitsch place *"If I Were a Bird"* next on his programme? It formed a contrast indeed, and is a charming piece withal. It is splendid practice, too, in sixths and fourths, for accuracy in both hands, and should not be forgotten. On this occasion it was played lightly, with swiftness and with delicate nuances. Henselt was noted for his remarkable technic, and for a very poetical style of playing.

Paderewski has written charming music for the piano, but one seldom hears it performed in concert. These Variations form one of his important works. They contrasted well with other numbers of the programme we are considering, and brought it to a brilliant close.

VI

Schumann, *Fantasie in C;* Chopin, *Barcarolle; Nocturne, Op. 62, No. 1; Valse, Op. 42; Two Etudes; Polonaise, A flat;* Brahms, *Ballade, Op. 10, No. 2; Valse; Paganini Variations.*

Whatever Friedman plays is filled with contrast, variety, nuance, style. He has a virtuoso technic of the highest order; the most difficult tasks are as nothing in his hands. One might classify him with Cortot and Bachaus, for all three have an almost superhuman piano mechanism. Yet each one is different in temperament, in *spirit.* Cortot is perhaps at home in more styles of composition; Bachaus is especially sympathetic with Schumann and Brahms, and the great masters of the German school. Friedman is a fine interpreter of Chopin, also Brahms and Schumann, to which he lends lightness and fantasy. He has not the serene repose for some of Mendelssohn's "Songs without Words," for instance, or for some movements of Beethoven's Sonatas. But in his own realm, the realm of fancy, imagination, nuance, he is supreme.

A peculiarly fitting programme for Friedman's

great gifts was the one noted above. From first to last he was unique, like no one else. Let a close student of the piano and its literature watch this artist in action. Playing with the greatest ease, with loose arm, relaxed weight and all that—as a matter of course—he has an untold number of movements of hand, arm and fingers, with which to express the effects he desires to produce. For power he uses heavy arm weight, reinforced by muscles of shoulders and back. He is fond of making the tone suddenly swell in passages and phrases, bringing the weight of body on the hands. For delicacy he has a whole bagful of surprises; his trills can be of gossamer lightness, little phrases and passages are often simply brushed over, with the lightest flutter of fingers. Yet the tones are all there, in miniature.

For all his lightness and delicacy, he gave the Schumann a most satisfying interpretation. The themes of the *Allegro* were sung with intimate understanding; the *March* was commanding in its power and sweep, while the *Andante* was truly expressive. The German and Polish ideas of expressiveness differ. Friedman lent a lightness and grace to many a passage, where a German artist would think first of solidity. Every first rank artist plays this work; no two play it in the same way. Schumann had something of the capricious and elfish in his make-up, and Friedman is able to enter peculiarly into the spirit of Schumann through his own temperament and adaptability.

The Polish artist, as has been said, is entirely at home in the music of Chopin. He began the Chopin group with the *Barcarolle,* so unique among the works of the master. Here were limpid tones, absolute smoothness in runs and ornaments, liquid trills and rich power for chords. If you are watching him, you must not forget to observe the pedaling. There is constant shifting of feet; usually both are working at the same time. Such pedalplay is of itself a great art.

At the sixth page of the *Barcarolle* a fine climax was worked up to the *Piu Mosso,* where chords were sonorous and powerful. The running passages toward the close were smooth as oil, and ended in a couple of strong chords.

The *Nocturne, Op. 62, No. 1,* which has been called the "Tuberose Nocturne," came next, seemingly almost a continuation of the same mood—of soulful sweetness. The melody was smooth and singing, the run at bottom of first page had the *crescendo* and *diminuendo* effect. At change of key, the new theme was brought out, almost like an improvisation. The following trills were clear as crystal; when played like that they are beautiful in themselves. Many of us remember with what pearly limpidity they fell from Paderewski's fingertips also. At the last line the short phrases alternated like question and answer, thus indicated and made clear by varied qualities of tone.

Of course the familiar *A-flat Valse* was dashed off in bravoura style. Just this contrast was needed to vary the almost cloying sweetness of the Nocturne.

A further antidote came with a couple of the Etudes. Op. 10, No. 5, the "Black Key Study." Was it ever done with lighter or more airy touch? And did you notice the little downward run, near the end of third page, was taken in glissando octaves, and with the most velvety touch?

In contrast with this delicacy came the *"Revolutionary Etude," Op. 10, No. 12,* with its thunders, tempered somewhat softer in spots for contrast.

After this familiar Etude was set a little-known Ballade of Brahms. It was the second of the four comprising No. 10, and one not so tuneful or stirring as either the first or third of the set. The opening is in octaves and extended chords, whose top notes carry the melody. Then follows a *"Doppio movimento,"* in quicker tempo, though not so quick as to lose the rhythmic design. The portion in 6/4 measure is lightly staccato, with the melody well brought out. In the last line, before change of key, the bass tones resemble ghostly trumpets. The first portion returns and the last three lines, forming the coda, are very soft. Brahms must have had some mood or impression in mind, of which this *Ballade* is the expression. As he has left no word concerning it, we can make our own story.

Now follows the little *Valse, No. 15, of Op. 39,* into which Friedman has woven the themes of the final Valse of the set—No. 16.   This little piece never fails to make an instant appeal, through its naive charm.

Friedman is especially sympathetic with the brilliant side of Brahms, and his performance of the *Paganini Variations* was sensational in its sweep and power, its rhythmic pulse, its play of nuance, and variety of tone.   Such glissando octaves! Such velocity in the most difficult passages.   It was absolute mastery of everything—down to the smallest details—that is possible in modern pianism.

VII

AN AFTERNOON WITH HAROLD BAUER

Beethoven, *Sonata, Op. 110;* Brahms, *Two Inter-mezzi; Ballade, G minor; Capriccio, B minor; Valses, Op. 39;* Chopin, *Sonata, Op. 58;* Schumann, *"Scenes from Childhood."*

"Bauer is one of the most satisfying pianists," is a remark frequently heard, in regard to this artist. He is a player to whose recitals serious students flock in large numbers. They come primed for the occasion, with plenty of "score" under arms or in portfolios. They know it will be well worth their while to follow a long and exacting recitation of some of their favorite pieces, as they will be sure to capture many points of interpretation. For Bauer is a deep musical thinker, a sane and introspective pianist. I believe I am right in saying he does not care to be known as a piano virtuoso, for that is evidently not his aim. He does not dazzle, nor amaze, nor sweep one away. He holds the music itself up before you and asks you to enjoy it with him. That is one of the charms of his playing; he seems to find his own pleasure in it. And you can lean back in your chair, free to find your own pleasure, too, in the music, as it unrolls before you.

"Do artists always play their pieces in the same way?" is a question often asked. Paderewski claimed the true artist should always do so. He said if he had thought out the conception of a work, it was his duty as an artist to reproduce that idea in the same way each time. Other pianists have a different way. Bauer, for instance, says emphatically he never plays twice exactly alike. "How is it possible to do so? I am a different man today from what I was yesterday, and tomorrow I shall not be the same as I am today."

All this may be a refinement of terms, which, sifted down, can mean much the same thing. Be this as it may, the afternoon on which Bauer devoted to expounding the meaning of one of his piano programmes, gave solid pleasure to the listeners, who departed with the conviction of having had a rare intellectual and musical feast.

And what he played for us that day was: Beethoven, Op. 110; a group of Brahms; Chopin *Sonata, Op. 58,* and the *Kinderscenen* of Schumann.

When we listened to the Beethoven Sonata, we felt it was Bauer at his best, because he made us feel the greatness of Beethoven. Such clearness of form and shape set the great work before us in all its noble simplicity. The opening was soft and quiet, the quicker movement crisp and bright. The slow movement was tender, like a voice speaking, sometimes sorrowfully, then with quiet resignation. The fugue which followed was so clearly and cleanly articulated, it could have been written down as we listened.

The Brahms group contained two *Intermezzi, Ballade in G minor,* the familiar *Capriccio in B minor,* and two-thirds of the *Valses, Op. 39.*

And first the *Capriccio.* Every student of the piano should study this delightful bit of gaiety; some well-known teachers make it obligatory. It is Brahms at his happiest. And note its effect on an audience. It brings smiles and restful looks to the faces of the listeners. Here is a study in lightest staccato, punctuated by accents and delicate nuances. No stiffness in wrist or arm may interfere with its lightness and fluency. It must have capriciousness, too, a quality it does not often get from its interpreters. The middle portion, pages three and four, seem to picture a beautiful landscape, which reveals new beauties the oftener we hear it. It is too often played "straight along," without those little tempo-nuances which make it fascinating. Why cannot players learn to "dwell on beautiful details"? If they only would, the pleasure of the listener would be enhanced an hundredfold.

Now we come to the Valses. Various pianists have shown us, in recital, how delightful they are. But we never get them all, more's the pity! This time ten out of the sixteen.

Of course Number 1 must start the group, with its octave passages full of crisp vigor. Then Number 2 in more dreamy mood; No. 3 with delicate coquetry and No. 4 in more pompous vein.

The *Sixth Valse, in C sharp,* was a model of crisp staccato and captivating delicacy. What a capital study it provides for skips, free arm and loose wrist. Let not the young player be deterred from undertaking it on account of its difficulties. All will yield to slow, careful practice of the right kind.

Valse No. 7 came next, a dreamy, langorous little piece, which this time did not seem so dreamy as at other times, because the pianissimos took on more life and tone. No. 8 was played slowly and softly, with considerable ritard on the eighth and fourteenth measures of the second division. A skip was now made to *Valse No. 12,* which resembles so strongly one of the songs of Brahms that we always wish words could be joined to it. Then came No. 14, played in spirited fashion, with varied strong, highlights.

After this came the most familiar one of all, the lovely Valse in A flat. In this the pianist made a little individual point. At the tonic, about the middle of fourth line, he inserted the final Valse, No. 16, in E major. When that was over he returned to the *Valse in A flat,* at the place where he had left it, and finished it. The effect was interesting and unusual.

The Chopin *Sonata, Op. 58,* received a thought-ful and beautiful interpretation. The *Scherzo* in particular was full of light and shade; the first and third parts light and swift, the middle portion slow and impressive. The *Adagio* was deeply felt and full of meaning, while the *Finale* abounded in life and vitality.

And lastly came those descriptive gems of Schumann, the *"Scenes from Childhood,"* which Bauer re-creates so inimitably. These ever-changing mood pictures are the delight of the imaginative artist, and have appeared a number of times in our concert halls. Mr. Bauer plays them with evident enjoyment, and this feeling is communicated to the listener. Two minor points to remember. All repeats are observed, and there are sufficient pauses between the numbers to insure the completeness of each little piece by itself.

The theme of Number One sings above the soft, smooth undercurrent of accompanying tones. A pause after the ritard in sixth measure of second part, creates a break before the sixteenth note, leading to the return of first theme is played.

The *Curious Story* is crisp and bright, with a break in eighth measure, after second beat. At third and fifth measures of second half, the tenor voice is made prominent. The same points are made a little later.

In No. 3, *Blind Man's Buff,* the pianist used a light, detached staccato, like the slapping touch em-

ployed by the French school. This touch gave the
light, dancing effect required.

The Entreating Child, No. 4, was indeed appealing, with its plaintive melody and subdued accompaniment.   The *ritardando,* indicated for four
measures, was modified to two, in the first instance.

No. 5, *Happy Enough,* was gay and bright.
When the theme was imitated in bass, as in second
and fifth measures, there was always a *crescendo.*
This was the case whenever these four tones appeared. At the close a pause.

An Important Event, No. 6, was given just the
right air of importance and pomposity, with strong
accents and *forte* and *fortissimo* power. The final
three measures received added emphasis, with a
corresponding ritard.

A tiny gem was the *Traumerei* (Dreaming),
played so simply and tenderly. Much soft pedal was
used.   At sixth measure the chord was broken in
both hands; the same at each recurrence. Each
artist plays this little piece in a slightly different
way.   Joseffy is remembered to have rolled the
dotted half notes in first measure, and every time
afterwards. The effect was a sort of shimmer of
harmony, which no one else has exactly reproduced.

In No. 8, *At the Fireside,* a prominent musician
suggested to the writer that the top notes of left
hand might be exchanged with lowest notes of
right, to facilitate the stretches, whenever possible.
This plan will overcome digital difficulties, as any
player can see for himself.

The Rocking Horse, No. 9, always evokes a broad smile from the audience, so absolutely is the movement imitated. The touch, too, is especially wooden and precise, with strong, rhythmic accents in bass, to give the rocking effect. No one plays this with quite the same effect Mr. Bauer creates.

A little poem is *Almost too Serious,* No. 10 with its many gentle ritards and pauses, its subdued tints. It is set between the jolly *Rocking Horse* and *Frightening,* No. 11. This was full of sudden changes necessary for the story. It must have been a ghost story, as it begins very softly, swells at fifth measure, with accents on three chords, also accents in eighth measure. Next comes the real ghost, the cause of all their fear, for all the children scamper to hiding. The right hand is very light staccato, while the left is legato, with accents on upper A and F natural. These portions are repeated several times through the piece.

Child Falling Asleep, No. 12, another dream number, which requires tenderness and delicacy. At the entrance of the E major section, the right-hand chord was broken. Occasionally a single tone was prolonged, to give the dreamy effect, and at the close there was a very long pause, before the *Poet Speaks.* He spoke very meditatively, as though he stood back, like a painter, to view the effect of his tender pictures of childhood's moods and fancies.

And thus regarding them, he fell into a reverie, where we reluctantly left him.

VIII

A RECITAL BY MYRA HESS

Brahms, *Sonata, Op. 5;* Schumann, *Papillons, Op. 2;* Frank Bridge, *The Dew Fairy;* John Ireland, *Ragamuffin;* Granados, *Alborada del gracioso;* Chopin, *Three Mazurkas, Ballade, Op. 23.*

Before the English pianist came to America (1921) her teacher, Tobias Matthay, the famous pedagogue and musician, of London, sent the present writer a letter, announcing the advent of his favorite pupil. The letter was couched in glowing terms. He considered Miss Hess the greatest woman pianist of the day, as she was the most musical personality he had ever known.

This was high praise and difficult to live up to. When Miss Hess appeared, she proved to be a charming pianist, though not exactly of the virile type. Her playing seemed to lean more to the delicate and gracious side and not to be quite equal to the broader and more emotional effects required in the greater piano music.

But on her second visit she seemed to have developed into a big artist, with splendid technical equipment, plenty of power, and a certain joyous buoyancy added to her delicacy and clarity. Her playing closely resembled that of Novaes in variety of nuance and tonal color. The same clarity, rhythmic perfection, soulful pedaling and artistic interpretation. If she has not quite reached the sonority and intensity of the young Brazilian, no doubt these will also be hers when she desires them.

A programme of her second season began with the Brahms *Sonata in F minor, Op. 5.* Composed in the flush of youthful energy, and enthusiasm, this third sonata of Brahms, in its wide range of expression, seems to mirror many sides of life. It is Mason who says: "Like Bach and Beethoven, Brahms spanned the whole range of human interests; deep feeling fills his music with primitive expressiveness, and at the same time great intellectual power gives it the utmost complexity.

In presenting so complex a work the player needs versatility as well as intellectuality. Miss Hess possesses both. With all her innate gentleness, she is able to project a theme in vivid colors. The virility with which she gave out the stirring opening phrases of the first movement, made a startling effect. The chords and skips were so brilliant and *sure.* The soft passage following the first outburst was calm and tender. So was the theme beginning middle of second page, and continuing to double bar. In the working out, all the themes were clearly set forth, with exact phrasing, nuance and variety of tone. There was nothing obscure; all stood revealed in appropriate form and tint.

The *Andante* mirrors a tenderly-sweet love song, and was played in that spirit, though at a somewhat slower tempo than the movement is usually conceived. The tones of the melody were of ravishing sweetness, and the accompaniment was never obtrusive, but always within the picture. This *Andante* is a long and discursive movement, and towards the close it rises to an impassioned climax of intense feeling, which soon subsides to a murmur of blissful content.

Following this ecstatic dream, the exuberant *Scherzo* bursts upon the ear. How buoyant those up-rushing scale figures, and the pulsing rhythm of the dance. The little descending groups of tones filling each measure of second page, were clear as little silver bells. Try to make them sound that way, and you will get the effect.

The *Trio* was lovely in its subdued tints. A return to the first portion brought back all the gaiety, crispness and incisive rhythms which the pianist knew so well how to portray.

After this fascinating *Scherzo* comes a short movement of two pages. It is an *Intermezzo,* which the composer tells us is a "glance backward," doubtless to the lover's happy meeting as pictured in the *Andante,* as the theme has something of the same contour. There are sharp contrasts here of loud and soft—it is a dream within a dream, and has a mysterious close. The tones are so charged with emotion that it is almost a relief when the *Finale* is reached.

This final *Allegro* is played with a joyous crispness, many dainty accents and nuances. The player proved herself equal to portraying the various mood changes, the swift passing from soft, dreamy passages to bright, buoyant chords and octaves. It was a noble work, beautifully set forth, without one obscure spot to mar its completeness.

In the Schumann *Butterflies,* Miss Hess was even more individual. She imparted to these charming pictures an airy lightness and delicacy they seldom receive. They were humorous, capricious, dreamy and gay by turns. No matter how airily she played, every note was there in its place. It often seemed as if her fingers scarcely touched the keys, yet the sounds were in their places. There was power, too, and heavy touch when necessary, as in No. 3, with octaves. The six strokes of the clock rang out at the close, then the uproar of the Carnival died away and soon all was still.

The third group of pieces on this programme contained *The Dew Fairy,* by Frank Bridge, a melodious, airy bit, followed by John Ireland's *Ragamuffin.* This is bright, whimsical, with distinctive rhythmic figures. It had to be played twice. Granados' *La Maja et le Rossignol* was longer and proved rather discursive. Ravel's *Alborada* finished the group. Here Spanish atmosphere was joined to French elegance and dexterity. On it

Miss Hess employed her most airy touches, her most ethereal colors. Her *glissando* runs pearled and rippled; they were marvels of smoothness.

The last quarter of the programme was devoted to Chopin, and this proved an excellent arrangement. Most artists place Chopin somewhere in the middle and add Liszt or perhaps some very bombastic numbers to close. Miss Hess chose to send her listeners away filled with the poetry of the greatest piano master of them all.

The lovely Mazurkas she chose fell on the ear with the charm of freshness after the complicated harmonies of some of the moderns. The *F sharp minor Mazurka,* from early Op. 6, is very melodious. It was played with characteristic buoyancy, with needful accent and stress in the right places. The second half, where the grace notes precede each chord, the music seemed to give a vivid vision of country couples dancing. It was played in that spirit of gaiety and vigor.

It is related of Leschetizky that he once remarked on the difficulty of conveying just the right spirit in Schumann. "Either you can play Schumann's music or you cannot," was his verdict.

It has always seemed that something of the same gift is required to interpret Chopin, especially the Chopin of the Mazurkas. They so intimately reflect the social life of the people, they are so elegant, so courtly, so dreamy and vigorous by turns. Many pianists play them but few seem to catch their true spirit. These dances must have marked rhythms yet always be somewhat capricious. The English pianist seemed to grasp this elusive quality of style to a remarkable degree, and gave a very satisfying reading of the national dances.

The second *Mazurka* was one of the several in A minor—Op. 67, No. 4—and one of the most charming of all. It is full of coquetry, of swift changes from winning sweetness to vigorous gaiety. The player seemed to have endless little nuances to enhance the beauty of her tones.

For the third she chose that lively dance in D major, Op. 33, No. 2. Its whirling figures, now in D and then in A—now loud, then echoing softly, suggest the merriest kind of movement. It is full of vitality, of lively wit and shifting motion. To give the true Polish swing, an accent is frequently used on the third beat, probably indicating a stamp of the dancer's foot. The whole was played with infectious gaiety and with an exuberance that was compelling.

And now came the beautiful *Ballade in G minor,* beloved of all budding aspirants for pianistic conquests. If they were among the listeners—as doubtless many of them were—they heard a rendering that was full of sentiment, yet quite free from exaggeration or sentimentality.

The Introduction was neither too loud, too soft, nor too dreamy; it was a just balance of all these. At *Moderato* the theme started slowly and very softly, gradually gaining somewhat in tone. At the fifteenth measure the little theme in bass peeped out, as counter-subject to the right-hand theme. The short cadenza on second page was velvety soft. The player also has the gracious gift of varying a repetition of any phrase, in tone or coloring. She kept the whole work in controlled and rather subdued tones, till the seventh page, where the theme returns in chords and sixths. Here all became *vivo* and *ff,* gradually falling off in power to the *Meno Mosso.*

Again the soft, dreamy theme, which soon worked up to a passionate climax, leading to the *Presto con fuoco.* Begin this softly, which will give greater contrast in working up. The tempo is rapid, with crisp, rhythmic accents. The runs on last page are brilliant, with big crescendos. The chords between are *piano,* but finally molded; each tone a little different in color. The final octave passage is very heavy, but starts slowly, gradually acquiring high speed, and finishing in a grand sweep of power and triumph.

GUIOMAR NOVAES—A COMPOSITE PROGRAMME

Bach, *Prelude and Fugue, D major;* Cesar Franck, *Prelude, Chorale and Fugue;* Chopin, *Barcarolle; Mazurka, Op. 67, No. 4; Etude, No. 25, No. 12;* Blanchet, *Two Preludes, Op. 10;* Vallon, *Harlequin;* Stojowski, *Chant d'Amour;* Mendelssohn, *Scherzo;* Liszt, *Thirteenth Rhapsodie.*

A piano recital by Guiomar Novaes is, for several reasons, an event. It is sure to be unique. It is bound to be as unlike other recitals as the giver's art differs from that of other recitalists. Critics and writers have endeavored to analyze this art, have tried to tell in just how far the admired Brazilian's pianism is perfected, intuitional mechanism and how far it is real genius. One critic expresses his conviction that she "plays the piano by the grace of God."

When we listen to a recital by her, we cannot help noting the absolute freedom and daring of her movements, the perfect adjustment and balance of relaxed weight, the digital mastery. We see the results of this mastery in an almost limitless variety of color and shading, a marvelous tonal gradation, from the finest spun *pianissimo* to the greatest resonance and power. What a boon to the younger generation of pianists, if they could know just how these things are accomplished. But Novaes cannot put the causes of these results in words. Though she seems to have good reasons for making the movements and exercising the physical conditions she employs, she cannot exactly explain the why and wherefore. Is it then the genius of technic which she possesses? Some of our foremost artists claim this gift as an early asset. All of them, however, had to perfect the gift before it was worthy to reflect the highest forms of pianistic art.

Admitting that Mme. Novaes was blest with a natural technic, she has developed it in a remarkable degree; she has developed it in special ways that no other pianist, except Paderewski, has thought of doing. In the line of sonorous tone, who can draw a sound of greater roundness and fulness, or one of more massive power? Who has more warmth of tonal quality, more lightness, more delicacy, or a more velvety touch?

As the pianist herself does not go into word-details, it remains for someone who has watched and followed her work many times, who has studied her playing from the moment she first appeared in the United States, to set down a few of the outstanding facts.

In searching for the cause of both the enormous power and the velvety quality of her tone, the vital source seems to be a correct understanding of re-

laxation. Now we know this is a very much mis-
understood word; we realize, too, there are various
kinds of relaxation. Every pianist claims he understands the right kind, when in reality he may have
little notion of it. The sort of relaxation Guiomar
Novaes possesses is the sort which brings greatest
results. It is the kind that can be detected in every
move, by those who understand. She plays with
absolutely relaxed weight. This weight is used with
infinite variety, both for ponderous chords—or
single tones—to the warm, velvety-soft passages. It
accompanies the continuous drop on the keys and
gives the quality she seeks. Other pianists may
push, punch, press or hit the keys, but Novaes
caresses them with relaxed weight. She has solved
the secret, either intuitively or consciously, of the
use of weight and its results. She can play in no
other way.

The various movements made by the pianist
grow out of the principle of weight. There is
nothing jerky, square or angular. All is poised,
balanced, curved, indeed the perfection of grace.
"Curved is the line of beauty," in her case. Those
big, rotary movements for chords and octaves give
accuracy with good tone. If both hands are needed
at opposite ends of the keyboard, the hands move
precisely together, with the same accuracy of curve
and sweep. What other player thinks of so small
a detail? There are no small things when an artistic effect is sought. And so with all the other

movements which are so individual with this artist; all the little taps, pats, caresses; they each and all come under the law of balance, weight, poise and control.

How does Novaes employ these principles when applied to interpretation? She is like a sculptress, molding the plastic tones of her instrument into idealized forms. Has she thought out all the wonderful effects she makes, or are they the inspiration of the moment? Both. She surely prepares her pieces with the greatest care, not sparing herself in any way. Yet, when before an audience, a highly sensitive condition is engendered; she becomes *en rapport* with her listeners and they with her. Outwardly calm and composed, the young artist throws herself absolutely into her work. She is for the time being, the absorbed interpreter, the messenger, to preach the evangel of beautiful tone, of spiritual meaning, unconscious of all but the message she delivers with such intensity and sweetness.

The first number on her programme, Bach *Prelude and Fugue in D major,* edited by Emanuel Moor, once her teacher, proved how inspiring Bach can be made when adequately played. Every theme was distinct and well balanced. The heavy portions, while ponderous and often played with arm thrown upon the keys and fingers of the utmost firmness, were never hard or brittle. All were molded and fused into an artistic whole.

In the *Prelude, Chorale and Fugue,* by Cesar

Franck, the pianist was in a deeply poetic mood. She sang the lovely theme softly and tenderly; the *Chorale* was uplifting, and the *Fugue* clear and beautiful.

More intense was the Chopin *Barcarolle.* This began softly, but gradually gained in power. The trills, single and double, were clear and rhythmic, like the twittering of birds. A long *crescendo,* begun before the *Tempo Primo* at change of key, reached a high degree of intensity at the *Piu Mosso* where it became *fortissimo.* Here it continued to grow in power, until the piano itself seemed unable to contain the passion of it. A pean of love, sung by two voices blending in exalted ecstasy—young love triumphant. Those who listened will never forget the thrill of it; those moments were indescribable; it seemed piano music had soared to the zenith of its demonstration.

A sweet, tender *Mazurka* followed the *Barcarolle* and then came the tremendous *Etude in C minor, Op. 25, No. 12.* Here again came wave upon wave of sonorous tone, as those double arpeggios surged up and down the keyboard, supporting the majestic theme. No trace of stiffness was there, as arms moved with the utmost freedom; not only arms but body was free also. It was electrifying. An added number was Chopin's *Prelude, No. 8,* played with rare lightness and grace. Many pianists avoid this Prelude. The melody should be sustained, while the accompaniment of arabesques should be *leggiero,* or "slapped."

The concluding numbers were lighter in character. Two *Preludes from Op. 10,* by the Swiss composer, Blanchet, were very pleasing. They were played without pause between and were followed by a pretty conceit called *Harlequin,* by Vallon, all light, dainty staccato. Splendid practice for hands inclined to stiffness. In these days stiffness in arms or wrists is tabooed, and cannot exist where right understanding of mechanism and movement obtains.

Stojowski, in a box, heard his *Chant d'Amour* interpreted most poetically. An impassioned climax before the return of the first theme was memorable. For power, sonority and daring, it equalled the climax of the Barcarolle.

And now comes one of the pianist's most dazzling achievements, the *Scherzo,* from Mendelssohn's *"Midsummer Night's Dream."* Was ever heard such sparkling delicacy, swiftness, smoothness and mastery? Each note in its place, every accent played with just the right stress, *crescendos* and *diminuendos* just where they ought to be—no more, no less. It was all like rare, filmy lace. Those white fingers seemed to flash over the keyboard of their own volition; but we knew the calm, sane mentality back of them governed every move. Such exquisite art is indeed an object lesson. Think how many repetitions must be made before such flawless

smoothness can be reached.   What care, thought,
patience, slow practice must have been bestowed
upon those figures and arabesques, before they
could take such shape and form.   An artist, no
matter how great, must be willing to go through
those stages to reach perfection.

The *Hungarian Rhapsodies* of Liszt fill a place
that no other music seems to occupy.   They are
usually expected to put the climax of virtuosity to
an otherwise severe programme.   To this end they
have fulfilled their mission endlessly.   Even if they
are not deep and learned, they are harmonious, vital,
poignant, and always make an eloquent appeal.
They form an effervescent dessert after a serious
repast.   A decade ago it used to be the *Second
Rhapsodie* that set the pulses tingling and feet tap-
ping to its infectious rhythms.   Then came the
Twelfth to frequent hearing.   Why do not artists
try some of the others?

Novaes chose the Thirteenth, into which she put
all the variety of touch and tone, of nuance and
mysterious meaning; some of the Magyar wail
which alternates with the frenzied joy of gypsy
dancing.

When a Liszt Rhapsodie is played like that, it
ceases to be mere display and becomes charged with
significance.   Even the cadenzas and passages can
be made delightful as vehicles for beautiful tones
and poetical nuance.

The piano will yield its secrets to those who seek

diligently for them.   And those secrets are worth the seeking.   The admired artist who has just re-created this music for us, thus giving us unforget-table moments of artistic refreshment, has discov-ered the key which unlocks the soul of the piano, and has rightly earned her place among the immor-tal interpreters, a "pianist by the grace of God."

ONE-COMPOSER PROGRAMMES

It is a much-discussed question whether or not one-composer recitals are advisable or advantageous, either to the artist or the audience. It is claimed by some there cannot be sufficient variety in the work of a single composer to warrant using his music exclusively during a long and taxing programme; that listeners weary of one style of music long before the end of a recital is reached, and other objections of a like nature. Yet artists continue to give one-composer programmes, and generally win success with them. Smaller players, with less command over the instrument—with far less mental control and resource—try to emulate the great ones, and fail, more or less conspicuously. So that one is forced to the conclusion that it is possible to compile a list of contrasting numbers from a few of the greatest masters, but not at all easy to present these in such a way that there shall be abundant variety of mood and meaning.

First, then, what composers can stand such a difficult test? Begin with Bach, the source and mainspring of greatness in our art. Can a pianist, without the aid of other instruments, or the human voice, present a programme of the grand old master, that shall have contrast enough, in the performance, not to weary a musical audience? You will grant it must be an exceptional player who can accomplish this feat. Those who have listened to the Bach programmes by Ernest Hutcheson know he can arrange a list of this music and interpret it with skill, with ample variety of touch and tone. It would be difficult to name five or even three others who have done the same. Siloti and Dohnanyi are acknowledged Bach players of renown, but neither have appeared in solo recitals of Bach's music. Siloti arranged a programme of Sonatas with the assistance of flute and violin, but has not, to the writer's knowledge, performed a programme of Bach for piano alone.

Take Beethoven. He who developed the sonata with such transcendent mastery, who so greatly welded the classic and romantic periods, can furnish forth various programmes, chosen from among the thirty-eight sonatas alone, to say nothing of the various sets of variations and pieces in lighter vein. Beethoven has inspired many a pianist to play his music for a whole programme, from von Bülow, whose performance of the "Last Five Sonatas," has become historic to many others who have come after him. Not so long ago Mme. Olga Samaroff performed the entire thirty-eight, in a series of five afternoons; a feat as rare as it is remarkable. Hutcheson, Gabrilowitsch, D'Albert, Elly Ney, Buhlig, and many others have given Beethoven programmes with the success proportionate to their mastery of the subject.

The next composer whose music lends itself readily to a complete programme is Schumann. From his richly prolific period of piano compositions, comprised between Op. 2 and Op. 28, it is possible to arrange a number of groups which will comprise great variety of form and meaning. Hutcheson selected three works only—*Kreisleriana, Kinderscenen* and *Etudes Symphoniques;* they filled an afternoon, and left nothing to be desired in the way of variety of content.

Two other composers might be named as able to stand the test—Brahms and Liszt. The Brahms recital will soon be with us. With the splendid *Sonata, Op. 5,* the *Rhapsodies, Capriccios, Intermezzi, Valses* and the dazzling *Paganini Variations,* together with the *Variations on a Handel Theme,* there is plenty of material for several lists.

A Liszt programme is occasionally heard; Arthur Friedheim, a pupil of Liszt, has played one or two. When the recital giver is able to include that masterpiece, the *B-minor Sonata,* it can be surrounded by various interesting and charming compositions.

But it is to Chopin that pianists turn most sympathetically when a one-composer programme is sought; Chopin, the greatest poet-composer for the piano who has thus far appeared. With his varied lists and styles of composition, it is comparatively easy to arrange half a dozen programmes, whose music shall, if properly interpreted, charm without wearying the listener.

If properly interpreted, did I say? That is the other half of the test. The music of the masters mentioned can prove engrossing, even thrilling, if interpreted by a master mind. For it is the mind after all, the sum of the mental qualities, the big grasp on the content of the composition, the colossal technic, masterful control, and power to project the meaning of the work, which makes a prodigious success; the lack of these qualities, or of some of them, tends to failure.

Before passing to the consideration of the Chopin Recital, a representative programme from each of the composers referred to is set down.

BACH, PLAYED BY HUTCHESON

English Suite, complete.

Five *Preludes and Fugues,* from *"Well-Tempered Clavier"*:

F minor, Part 2, No. 12.

B flat major, Part 1, No. 21.

E flat minor, Part 1, No. 8.

C sharp major, Part 1, No. 3.

E major, Part 2, No. 9.

Italian Concerto, Four Inventions:

E minor, C major, F major, F minor.

Chromatic Fantasy and Fugue.

SCHUMANN, PLAYED BY HUTCHESON

Kreisleriana, Op. 16.
Kinderscenen, Op. 15.
Etudes Symphoniques, Op. 13.

BEETHOVEN, PLAYED BY GABRILOWITSCH

Sonata, A major, Op. 2, No. 2.
Thirty-two Variations, C minor.
Rondo, G major.
Sonata, Op. 57.
Sonata, Op. 110.

BEETHOVEN, PLAYED BY HUTCHESON

Sonata, Op. 90, E minor.
Bagatelle, Op. 126, No. 4.
Minuet, E flat.
Rondo, Op. 129.
Sonata, Op. 57.
Sonata, Op. 111.

A BRAHMS PROGRAMME

Sonata, Op. 5.
Ballade, Op. 10, No. 3.
Intermezzo and Capriccio, Op. 76.
Rhapsodie, G minor.
Variations on Paganini Theme.

LISZT PROGRAMME, PLAYED BY HUTCHESON

Sonata in B minor.
Sonetto Petraca, 123.
Funerailles.
Concert Etude, F minor.
Legende, St. Francis Preaching to the Birds.
Rhapsodie, No. 13.

XI

THE CHOPIN RECITAL

Hunting in the garret one rainy afternoon, a regular treasure trove was discovered. An old letter book, containing masses of piano programmes, preserved for the last half century. Here were both European and American programmes of recitals, performed by men and women, then in their early youth, who are now our past masters in the art of piano playing.

Forty years ago programmes were planned much as they appear today. There is the diffuse style, where many composers are represented by one or two pieces each. This plan usually makes a lengthy list. It reminds one of a coat of many colors, as though the hearers must be diverted by constantly shifting moods and pictures. The concentrated style consists of the work of but two or three composers, or of a few lengthy compositions; the listener can then enter more closely into the thought of the masters presented.

In the earlier time there were "one-composer programmes" as well as now. D'Albert played his Beethoven, Friedheim his Liszt; Brahms interpreted his own massive works, then strange and new, but

222

now so clear and beautiful. Then came Paderewski, to conquer America as he had done Europe. His programmes were diffuse, embracing many styles. When he played a one-composer recital, he chose the music of Schumann and Chopin. There are two of these one-composer programmes on record, one each from the music of the masters named.

Along with Paderewski's advent we had de Pachmann, who always played Chopin for a single-composer recital. From my treasure book of programmes, I find he gave nearly a dozen recitals in New York of Chopin's music during his visits to us. These were doubtless repeated in other cities. Several of these lists included the *Sonata* of the *Funeral March,* and the big *Polonaise, Op. 53.* One programme will be noted here which contained neither.

CHOPIN PROGRAMME, PLAYED BY PADEREWSKI
IN 1900

Fantaisie, Op. 49.
Three Preludes, Nos. 15, 16, 17.
Two Nocturnes, Op. 37 and 62.
Sonata, Op. 35; Ballade, Op. 52.
Four Etudes, Two Mazurkas.
Valse, Op. 34, No. 1; Berceuse.
Polonaise, Op. 53.

CHOPIN PROGRAMME, PLAYED BY DE PACHMANN,
IN 1893

Allegro de Concert, Op. 46.
Barcarolle, Op. 60.
Fantaisie Impromptu, Op. 66.
Fantaisie, Op. 49; Scherzo, Op. 31.
Preludes, Nos. 15, 16, 19, 24.
Ballade, Op. 38; Mazurka, Op. 41-3.
Valses, Op. 64-2, and Op. 42.

Turning over programme records of more recent years, it is found there have been, roughly speaking, near a score of programmes devoted solely to the piano music of Chopin, given in New York, in one or other of the large concert halls. These have been played by Hofmann (2), Gabrilowitsch (4), Ignaz Friedmann, Bauer, Novaes, Hutcheson, Goodson, two each; and by Godowsky, Bachaus, Powell and Hughes, one each.

Generally the lists contained one Sonata, some had both. Most of the players used the beautiful *Fantaisie, Op. 49,* one of the most beloved of all compositions by the master. It is indeed not difficult to arrange an absorbing programme of Chopin's music, since there is such a variety of form and mood to draw from. Lovers of piano music have every opportunity to become thoroughly acquainted with the Pole's compositions. Not only are frequent Chopin recitals to be heard, but this music forms part of nearly every programme of piano music used in public, with hardly an exception.

Among the programmes of recent seasons, Harold Bauer's list contained *Sonata, Op. 58; Polonaise, Op. 44; Fantaisie, Op. 49; Ballade, Op. 38; Scherzo, Op. 39; Berceuse, Op. 57,* and a few smaller pieces. These were all delivered with the pianist's well-known mastery and insight.

A little later came a recital by Gabrilowitsch, who chose the *Sonata, Op. 35; Fantaisie, Op. 49; Ballade, Op. 47;* the fiery *Scherzo, Op. 20;* six *Preludes,* a *Nocturne* and some *Mazurkas.* These were all poetically and convincingly played.

Godowsky's list included the two Sonatas, the seldom-heard *Fantaisie Polonaise;* six *Preludes; Impromptu, Op. 29; Valse, Op. 42;* and the big *Polonaise, Op. 53.*

Katharine Goodson chose *Sonata, Op. 58;* seven *Etudes; Berceuse;* and a few *Valses.*

Novaes used the *Sonata, Op. 35; Fantaisie, Op. 49; Impromptu, Op. 36;* some *Mazurkas;* and the ever-familiar *Polonaise, Op. 53.*

Edwin Hughes placed both Sonatas on his programme, together with the *Fantaisie, Op. 49,* and some shorter numbers.

But all the foregoing is past history; let us come down to the present. During the New York season of 1922-3 there were given at least seven Chopin programmes. They were played by Hutcheson, Hofmann, Gabrilowitsch, Novaes, Powell, Bachaus and Friedmann. A comparison of the programmes offered by these artists would be deeply interesting to the pianist. It will be in the nature of an educational inspiration to the piano student to glance over these lists and note the special characteristics of each.

Mr. Hutcheson opened his programme with the great *Fantaisie, Op. 49,* that noble epic in tones. This was followed by the *Ballade,* which begins so gently and peacefully, until it becomes struck by a whirlwind of passion. Then fierceness and gentleness contend for the mastery, as is so often the case in this master's music. Now comes nine of the *Preludes,* a *Nocturne in F sharp,* the fiery *Scherzo, Op. 20,* and five *Etudes.* Fine as Mr. Hutcheson's interpretation of these compositions was, he seemed to surpass himself in the *Etudes.*

CHOPIN PROGRAMME, PLAYED BY HUTCHESON

Fantaisie, Op. 49; Ballade, F major.
Preludes, Nos. 20, 23, 21, 22, 3, 6, 7, 10, 16.
Nocturne, F-sharp minor; Scherzo, B minor;
Valse, E minor; Mazurkas, Op. 31, 1-2; Op. 68-2.
Etudes, Op. 10-8; Op. 25-5, 25-6, 7, 11.

CHOPIN PROGRAMME, PLAYED BY GABRILOWITSCH

Etude, E major.
Valse, Op. 34-2; Op. 42.
Sonata, Op. 35.
Preludes, Nos. 1, 4, 3, 7, 8, 15, 17, 19, 20, 23, 25.

Mazurka, Op. 33-4.
Nocturne, Op. 27-2.
Scherzo, Op. 20.
Encores were *Nocturne, Op. 15-1; Valse, E minor; Fantaisie Impromptu, Op. 66.*

The Russian pianist opened his recital with a deeply felt rendition of the elegiac *Etude in E major.* In it was expressed a wonderful calm. The player knows the value of the pause, both rhetorical and poetical. In this same spirit of calm came the *A minor Valse,* which was followed by the brilliant *A-flat Valse, Op. 42.*

Now came the *Sonata,* representing varied moods, some gay, others serious and exalted.

The selection of *Preludes* included all the favorites, even the little No. 7 had a place as well as the formidable No. 24. This was taken at high speed and was full of fire.

The D-flat Nocturne was tender and poetic, the Mazurka delicately capricious and the Scherzo brilliant and tender by turns.

CHOPIN PROGRAMME, PLAYED BY GUIOMAR NOVAES

Fantaisie, Op. 49.
Sonata, Op. 35.
Four *Preludes.*
Three *Etudes.*
Two *Mazurkas.*
Scherzo, C-sharp minor.

When this pianist announces a recital, we know it will prove a feast of good things. For the admired Brazilian has the rare power of filling the music she plays with intensity, with poetry, passion, delicacy and power. Her projection of the *F-minor Fantaisie* was full of tonal variety, of color, of imagination.

The Sonata is one of her masterpieces of delineation; each time she does it, the work seems a new creation, so spontaneously is it projected. That is the secret of great piano playing; it should be a "new created world," at every performance.

The Preludes were full of contrast of tone and color. The Etudes were brilliant and the lovely Mazurkas dainty and capricious. The *Scherzo, Op. 39,* was a dramatic and highly finished performance of a great work.

CHOPIN PROGRAMME, PLAYED BY JOHN POWELL

Nocturnes, F-sharp minor, and *B major.*
Scherzo, E major.
Sonata, Op. 58.
Impromptu, Op. 36.
Barcarolle, Op. 60.
Etude, C-sharp minor, Op. 25.
Etude, C-sharp minor, Op. 10.
Allegro de Concert, Op. 46.

Mr. Powell began with the seldom heard *Noc-*

turne in F-sharp minor, gently elegiac in the first portion, somewhat more stirring in the middle portion. Someone has said of this portion, that at the recurring pair of chords, "a tyrant commands," while at the following figure "the others ask for mercy." If the second Nocturne had been replaced by a Mazurka, for instance, there would have been more variety in the first group.

The Sonata, though not so frequently heard as the one in B-flat minor, is an equally beautiful work, and was poetically played. The third group contained familiar numbers and the little known *Allegro de Concert* completed the list.

CHOPIN RECITAL, PLAYED BY IGNAZ FRIEDMAN

Sonata, Op. 58.
Berceuse, Op. 57; Mazurka.
Etudes, Op. 10, 5-7; Op. 25, 7, 8, 9.
Sonata, Op. 35.
Andante and Polonaise, Op. 22.

Ignaz Friedman included both Sonatas in his Chopin scheme, supplemented by five Etudes, the ever-familiar *Berceuse* and the *Andante Spianato and Polonaise.* With what stupendous mastery did he interpret these compositions, imbuing them with individual charm and true Polish spirit. His fingers seemed tipped with velvet; he caressed quite as much as he thundered. His work compels deep admiration, and grows more beautiful, more sympathetic, as time passes.

CHOPIN RECITAL, PLAYED BY WILHELM BACHAUS

> *Sonata, Op. 58.*
> *Berceuse, Op. 57.*
> *Polonaise, Op. 44.*
> *Nocturne, Op. 62.*
> *Barcarolle, Op. 60.*
> *Valse, Op. 34-1.*
> *Etudes, Op. 10, 2-3; Op. 25-11.*

Wilhelm Bachaus, the German master, gave an all-Chopin recital, with this programme. The technic for Chopin seems as easy as child's play for him. Like some of the other masters of the keyboard, his most compelling successes are often achieved through the Etudes. One of these, Op. 10, No. 2, a study in chromatic figures, which employ the third, fourth and fifth fingers almost exclusively, was taken at a whirlwind pace and won instant acclaim. It had to be played three times over to satisfy the enthusiasm, before the recital could proceed. The *"Winter Wind"* Etude, *Op. 25, No. 11,* which closed the list, caused another demonstration.

Three more Etudes were added, also the *Mazurka, Op. 50-3.*

It seems the work of this great artist grows deeper and more sympathetic each time he is heard.

CHOPIN PROGRAMME, PLAYED BY JOSEF HOFMANN

Polonaise Fantaisie.
Valse in A flat, Op. 64.
Fantaisie, Op. 49, F minor.
Twenty-four Preludes.
Impromptu, Op. 36, F sharp.
Mazurka, F-sharp minor.
Polonaise, Op. 53.

Perhaps it may be said, without the least reflection on the splendid achievements of the master pianists already mentioned, that thought turns with lingering satisfaction to the Chopin Programme rendered by Josef Hofmann. Let us dwell for a moment on his presentation of this Polish music, which should be especially sympathetic to him, being himself a Pole. He is indeed one of those great artists who can identify themselves completely with the composer they interpret. He has, of course, a great technic, with much variety of tonal shading, and can make the piano sing, whisper, or thunder like a full orchestra.

His programme opened with that strange, weird *Polonaise Fantaisie.* It has been said there is no greater test for the poet-pianist than this same Polonaise. It is lurid with tempest, yet there are a few soft lights and tender places in it. The charming *A-flat Valse* followed like a cool, refreshing breeze upon a fevered brow.

The *Fantaisie, in F minor,* never can be heard too often.   It is so rich in content and meaning, that some new angle of vision is opened up to the listener with each new reading.

The same may be said of the Preludes.   What a storehouse of poetic moods, of colorful impressions. The pianist gave the entire set, for which we were grateful, as many of the programmes contain but a few of these exquisite miniatures.

The *Impromptu* was alluring, full of variety and color.   So was the lovely *Mazurka in F-sharp minor.*

The *Polonaise* thundered mightily, and was taken at terrific speed.   Among the many encores that followed were several of other composers; among them the Liszt *Campanella* and the *Juggleress* of Moszkowski.

XII

PADEREWSKI AND THE CHOPIN PROGRAMME

Those who heard Paderewski on his first visit to America can never forget the sensation he created at that time. I can see him as plainly as though it were but yesterday, as he stepped upon the platform at Carnegie Hall, on the evening of his debut. How slender and young he looked, with that crown of golden locks. Everyone recalls how he walked slowly toward the piano, fingering his cuffs as he went. When seated on the low chair he always used, he looked more slight than ever. Before beginning to play he always gave a couple of crashing chords, with arms raised head-high, as if to call the listeners to attention.

The enthusiasm aroused that evening grew and grew; it spread country-wide, though the fountain head was in New York. Here the Polish artist played fourteen times the first season, and sixteen the second. This allowed his admirers opportunity to study minutely his remarkable pianism, his movements, his gradations of tonal coloring, nuances, fine *pianissimos* as well as thunderous *fortissimos*. It was a new world of technic he held up for our admiration, a technic of perfect control, of perfect

233

command, exquisite in tone quality.   But all this is past musical history.

What we have now to consider is the playing of the Paderewski of today, the work of the ripe artist, who has lived a whole lifetime of world-experience since that early period.

The question uppermost in everyone's mind is: How does he play now?   Has he lost or gained; is he as great as he was—or greater?   Is that beautiful tone quality preserved that we loved in the early artist, before anxiety and vicissitude sharpened the tone and rendered the touch at times harsh and discordant, "like sweet bells jangled"?

Each one who hears him now, on his return to the scenes of his former triumphs, will answer this question according to his own light and experience. I have just come from listening to his third and last New York recital, and will make my confession of impressions.

Is it not more than a mere coincidence that he should offer a Chopin programme for his farewell appearance in New York?   There had been seven Chopin recitals already, his made the eighth.   But in spite of a super-abundance of Chopin, the fame of the player as well as the music drew an audience that packed the great Hall from pit to dome.   Let us listen with the rest, not merely to be enthused and charmed, but to see how it is done, to get behind the notes to the meaning of the music and its manner of production; to note what sort of technic is required for this or that effect.

When Paderewski entered, half an hour after the appointed time, he looked out upon a sea of faces, expectant and reverent. Moved by a common impulse the great audience rose and remained standing till the artist was seated. Will people do that for any other pianist? You and I will sit quietly through the lengthy programme and will not leave till he has finished.

THE PROGRAMME

Fantaisie, Op. 49.
Preludes, Nos. 15, 16, 21, 24.
Nocturnes, Op. 15.
Ballade, A flat; Scherzo, Op. 31.
Barcarolle, Four Etudes.
Sonata, Op. 35.
Mazurka, Op. 17-4; Valse, Op. 42.
Polonaise, Op. 53.

The *Fantaisie* was noble in spirit, and unrolled before us like a story of old romance. The beginning was soft in tone quality: the theme, which soon enters, was sung with tenderness and beauty. Where the chord containing it was over an octave, it was slightly broken and dwelt upon. On the following page, where a passage twice ascends, a diminuendo effect was produced. The arpeggios were begun slowly, with pauses between. The song portion following was not taken too slowly. In the figurated portion in sixths and fourths, the melody sang in the upper voice. What we might call the Chant was slow and meditative, proclaimed with beautiful tone, for which the master is noted. The final phrases were clear and ringing at first, but gradually subsided to a quiet *piano*. When all was over we felt we had heard a beautiful tone poem, played just as we would like to have it played.

The group of four Preludes brought back old memories. No. 15 did not become sickly or sentimental; to avoid which the tempo was a little faster than some others take it. The middle section began softly, with a couple of fine crescendos in it, and very little if any ritard at return of first portion. The passage in single notes was clear and beautiful.

Prelude 16 was taken at a very rapid pace, with well-accented bass. Last chord heavy, with top note taken by thumb of left hand, over. No. 21 had the bass figure well articulated throughout, with a fine *crescendo* in the middle portion. Prelude 24 was big and dramatic all through, with melody in detached, arm-weight movements. The long runs had accents on top, while the final chords were like cannon booming.

The Nocturnes were both serene and lovely with expressive shadings.

And now came the familiar *Ballade in A flat*. Yet it was unfamiliar, too, in its wealth of fantasy, of nuance and color. It was a musical story, full of mood pictures; in fact, it seemed an exotic day dream, through which lordly knights and lovely ladies moved, loved and romanced. There was conflict, too, clash of arms, then surrender, peace, ecstasy, realization.

Scherzo, Op. 31. What a difference the pause, rightly placed, made in this well-worn piece. There were pauses after each of those little upward gusts of tone. There was restraint, too, in the right spots; no unseemly rush, for the sake of rushing. How poetical the song in the middle section; the return of the first portion was impressive and brilliant.

Into the *Barcarolle* Chopin seemed to pour the ardent romance of a lifetime, and his Polish interpreter revealed this spirit to us. He began the introductory measures with full, rich tone, which became softer when the theme entered. The melody was full of light and shade, the trills passionate, the cadenza-runs ended in *pianissimo*. The figurated passage work in right hand was accompanied by a bass that declaimed with intensity. The last runs were very expressive.

Etudes came next. The one in thirds was not taken as rapidly as some other players take it. What of that? Even Paderewski himself, in his youth, may have played it with greater speed. This time it was a thing of sheer beauty, without taking one's breath away. The next was Op. 10, No. 10—less familiar, but charming. The third, in C-sharp minor, was full of tonal variety and nuance. How poignantly that bass wailed and pleaded; its intensity would move a heart of stone. The finish was almost inaudible in its delicacy.

The A minor study, *"Winter Wind,"* closed the group. It was taken at high speed; the theme in left hand went crashing on through the stormy right-hand passage work. It was terribly exciting to watch and listen to. The ending was like the crack o' doom.

What can be said of the Sonata? It was tremendous all through. With the first chords the pianist marshalled his forces in triumph and the story began. How full of poetic fantasy were those phrases! All the pent-up forces of emotion, which had gathered since the beginning of the recital, seemed to burst upon us. The final chords of the first movement came straight from the shoulder, and taxed the endurance of the instrument, yet without harshness.

The *Scherzo* was brilliantly bright, with lurid flashes here and there. The ascending passage in thirds was, in effect, like one great sweep of sound, in which all individual tones melted. The middle section was sweet and entreating, and the measures containing the trill slightly ritarded.

The *Funeral March* began very softly and gradually rose to a big climax, though you will agree in wishing the tempo had been a little slower. The middle section was calm and sweet. The return to the first portion began with bass taken in a lower octave, as Hofmann does, which gives a strange, unearthly effect. It began *pianissimo* but increased in power. The final movement entered at once, with little or no pause, and was uncanny in its ghostly swiftness.

The *Mazurka* which followed has been designated as full of hectic despair. It was also full of tender sweetness. The *A-flat Valse* began with a trill *ff,* and was healthy and charming throughout.

In the *Polonaise, Op. 53,* the opening passage was followed by soft chords of lovely quality. The whole spirit of the piece was one of conquering command and triumphant accomplishment.

And after the Polonaise—what? The recital was over yet the people refused to leave. Some made the familiar rush for the stage, to obtain a nearer view of the wizard of the keyboard. But most of us sat quietly in our places, waiting for the after-feast which was sure to follow. It came in generous measure, sometimes three pieces at a time. Among them were: *Berceuse; G-flat Etude; Valse in C-sharp minor; Prelude in A flat; "Maiden's Wish";* and *Mazurka in D flat.*

The whole recital seemed the expression of an exalted mind, attuned, through life's experiences, to the highest and deepest emotions. And yet there was no sense of exaggeration, or striving for exotic and bizarre effects. It was pure music we heard, manifested through one who completely understood its meaning.

PART IV

A few artists and teachers have been asked to give their views on programme construction. Some have kindly responded to the request in writing, while others have expressed a thought or two verbally.

Among those who have stated the case of the Programme most fully, yet concisely, is Ernest Hutcheson. Mr. Hutcheson's article is placed at the top.

ERNEST HUTCHESON

"Programme-making is an art in itself. The mere putting together of a number of good compositions by no means constitutes a good programme. Attention must be paid to length, balance, unity, and to contrast of tempo, mood and tonality. The occasion, the audience for whom the programme is intended, even the hall in which it is to be given, should all be considered. The subject is so broad that I shall confine my remarks to the special matter of programmes for piano recitals.

In my opinion a concert exclusively of piano music should rarely exceed an hour and a half in length. This means about seventy to seventy-five minutes of actual playing, with allowances for pauses between groups and a few minutes' grace for possible applause.

"A program should not, as a rule, consist entirely of long, serious works, and by no means should it be constructed entirely of short pieces. The tonalities should be diversified, but preferably without violence of contrast. It should be remembered that the ear tires of slow *tempi* more quickly than of fast; hence a Sonata or Symphony of four movements contains usually only one *Adagio* or *Andante*. Lyrical and brilliant or dramatic moods should therefore be arranged in effective sequence. No heavy strain should be put on the listener's attention after the first hour of music.

Good programmes may follow out a particular idea or be more general in character. If the latter plan is chosen, the chronological sequence is most often favored and is always fairly safe in effect. An artist of good judgment, however, will often successfully depart from chronological order, by putting a serious modern work, such as a Brahms or Liszt Sonata early in the program.

"The pianist should not attempt too much, or try to represent too many composers in a single concert. On the other hand, one-composer programs are also dangerous, because contrast of style is difficult to secure; only the greatest masters of composition can be listened to with pleasure in this way.

"Encores during the course of a program are, I think, very disturbing, though a short piece may occasionally be repeated on demand of the audience without bad effect. The artist who wishes to be amiable (as of course most artists do) may add as much as he pleases at the end of the recital. This is purely a personal feeling, and I am far from criticizing those who think differently. In any case, encores should enhance the value and the enjoyment of a concert and not detract from it. The addition of less worthy music, often indulged in under the excuse of the encore, is nothing but a nuisance.

"Finally, *no music is too good for the public.* There is not the slightest occasion for any pianist to offer a "light," trivial programme to an unfamiliar audience anywhere in the United States or Canada, provided only that monotony is avoided. To be "played down to" is something that every audience rightly resents."

HAROLD BAUER

"I have made programmes of almost every conceivable style and form. I keep a typed record of each recital I have ever given, and as I turn the pages here, I see many that are planned in a conventional way, that is—beginning with Bach and ending with Liszt. Others contain the works of but a couple of composers, or are otherwise specially arranged.

"A programme I remember hearing during the past season, contained three long, heavy works, played one after the other, at the beginning. This would be called a poorly-planned programme, even though played by one of the greatest pianists of the time.

"A great orchestral conductor was in the habit of using several works of similar character on the same programme, to show how different composers looked at the subject from varied angles.

"Lately I was playing a recital which opened with a *Fantasie* of Mozart's followed by *Sonata, Op. 11,* by Schumann. While I went through the Mozart piece I was continually thinking I did not want to follow it with the Sonata. When I finished the first number I announced, that instead of giving the Sonata, I would play the Schumann *Fantasie in C, Op. 17*. Thus the two *Fantasies* were contrasted. We do not know what Mozart had in mind when composing his piece, but we *do* know what Schumann thought of, for he has told us.

"A well-arranged programme is in itself a work of art. It is like the movements of a sonata, which form a complete whole. Or it may be likened to a tree, whose trunk bears branches, leaves, flowers and finally fruit."

WILHELM BACHAUS

"Perhaps it is not so much contrast one should look for in a well-arranged programme, as balance, proportion and unity. We generally consider it best to place more serious works at the beginning, and the lighter, more brilliant pieces toward the end.

"It is interesting work to form a good programme, but one that requires a great deal of thinking, and much experience."

IGNAZ FRIEDMAN

'To make a good programme is a very difficult matter, for the artist, since so many things must be considered. In arranging a list of classics it may not be possible to always choose what one likes, because certain pieces will not group well with others. And again, some may be too severe for the audience; one has to think of that. Then, if it is desired to place modern compositions along with the classics, it needs fine taste and judgment to choose suitable works, that will go well together. Modern music for the piano is not nearly so difficult to master as classic literature."

ALEXANDER SILOTI

"It is a very difficult matter to plan a successful programme scheme. The general order seems to be to begin with Bach and end with Liszt or more modern composers.

An artist's programme seems to me a very individual thing. I would not arrange it in this way. I should like to put Bach at the end, or near it. He is always serious and earnest and his music would send the listener home with high, noble thoughts. Liszt should always come before Bach— and Chopin also—as I see it.

"We often see some of the greatest works of piano literature on the programmes of young, immature players. I do not discourage their learning the notes of these works, but they cannot yet begin to interpret them. They must have lived and suffered, in order to enter into these mighty thoughts. They must have reached middle life before they have gained the experience to deeply appreciate and enter into what is highest and best in our art."

GUIOMAR NOVAES

Naturally, the gifted Brazilian would consider programme building from the artistic rather than the educational side; and she is right, too. After three seasons in America and several tours in Europe, she has had wide experience and can speak with authority.

"Here are my programme books," she said, pointing to a pile of black covers. In this one, played in Geneva, Switzerland, I was a little girl of fourteen, with hair hanging down the back. Here, on this programme, played in Paris, there are but three numbers: Bach, *Prelude and Fugue in A minor* (for organ, arranged for piano by Liszt), the

Schumann *Symphonic Etudes* and the entire set of Chopin preludes.

"So many things have to be considered when making up a programme; the place, the hall, the mentality of the people, whether they have heard me before, the kind of music they appreciate, and so on. In smaller cities I play more genial music, for I feel it will be better understood. In New York, of course, I can give the stiffest kind of a programme; it can be very severe, though I always try, by skillful arrangement, not to have it seem heavy.

"When I must announce a programme months ahead, I work on the list for awhile. Perhaps after a month or so I change it; then another grouping suggests itself and I change again, sometimes up to almost the last moment. As to actual sequence of pieces, I try them over and over, in various positions to test which go best together, as to key and content, to preserve unity, yet have contrast and avoid monotony.

"I sometimes plan a conventional programme, from Bach to Liszt; then again I may reverse the whole thing. It does not seem wise to put the very heaviest work as a first number; rather lead up to it through one or two shorter pieces. Modern music comes last on the programme, as a general thing.

"You see I must travel with my programme books, so that I shall not repeat works in the same city or town. For a tour I must have at least two working programmes, though sometimes I need to substitute other numbers. For New York I need three or four programmes each season. I am constantly working on new things—novelties, or classics that I do not yet know. I do not remember how many pieces comprise my repertoire, for I have never counted them, though a list might be made up from programmes."

CLARENCE ADLER

"A well-arranged programme of piano music should tell a story. We have, in the beginning, the introduction of characters and their environment. The plot begins to show itself, then thickens; intensity increases; the climax arrives; conclusion follows. In such a way as this I would build a programme.

CARL ROEDER

"A programme of piano music is often arranged to suggest the development of our art from classic to modern. Or we might say the growth of piano music is indicated by periods. In arranging a programme into several groups, works should be associated which seem to harmonize—to go together, without too violent a contrast of style and content."

HAROLD RANDOLPH

*Director, Peabody Conservatory of Music,
Baltimore, Md.*

"As to my own views on Programme Building, I cannot help feeling that the prevailing plan upon which all our programmes are built is in the main a sound one. For it follows roughly that upon which the menu for a dinner is planned and takes full account of human limitations and requirements, namely: *hors d'oeuvres* or other preliminary to "get going," then a *pièce de resistance,* while appetite and general receptivity are at the maximum; then something of a more piquant flavor requiring less concentration, and finally a bit of froth to wind up. I confess that after a long, serious program *to which I have really listened,* I am only fit to respond to a rather superficial appeal at the end. As to a chronological arrangement, it seems to me of much less importance, for often the older composers are far less serious and make much less of a demand upon either our brains or emotions than some of the later ones.

"A Sonata is, roughly speaking, laid out somewhat in accordance with this scheme. First movement appeals to head, second to heart, third to feet, and the last is to send us home in a good humor.

"It is needless to say that in an over-sophisticated place like New York or Berlin, it is often desirable to stimulate the jaded appetite by reversing all this and doing the totally unexpected—even if it be somewhat abnormal and indefensible on other grounds. I am only describing what I think a sound principle for general guidance."

PEABODY DIPLOMA RECITAL, PLAYED BY ESTHER LOVE

Bach-Tausig, *Toccata and Fugue, D minor*.
Beethoven, *Sonata, Op. 110*.
Schumann, *Etudes Symphoniques*.
Chopin, *Ballade, G minor*.
Debussy, *Reflets dans l'eau*.
Liszt, *Tarantelle*.

WILLIAM LINDSAY

Department of Music, University of Minnesota.

"I have often asked myself why the recital programmes of today are so different from those of my student days. The first recital I ever heard was one by D'Albert, in 1896; a stereotyped program, commencing with the older classics, travelling up through the romanticists to the final display of *technique*. How different from the programmes of today.

"I think, if I were presenting a half-dozen pupils in recital, I would strive to give their individual style the limit of freedom. Those classically inclined should choose according to their own special gift. I have pupils who love Bach; others who really call for Beethoven.

"I never believe in long recitals. The mentality and 'sitting power' (!) is otherwise than in the old Leipsig days, when Lamond gave the 'Last Five' Sonatas to a crowded house, and Reisenauer could play for two and a half hours on a stretch."

SWEET BRIAR COLLEGE, VIRGINIA

MISS HELEN F. YOUNG,

Director, Department of Music.

"It seems to me that one's aim in arranging a student-recital programme is quite different from that of the artist. For his aim is primarily to interest an audience, and to that end he may search for the new, the unusual; even bizarre numbers will have their place. Whereas the student is a musician in the making, and his time has been occupied largely in getting acquainted with the best literature, rather than in exploring the less-known paths. Consequently the best type of student programme should, in my opinion, consist for the most part of works from the great masters, choice being given, of course, to composers and selections which appeal most to the temperament of the individual student.

"Programme from Sweet Briar College, played by Miss Selma Brandt:

"Bach, *Prelude and Fugue, B flat.*

"Beethoven, *Sonata, Op. 31, No. 3; Menuet and Allegretto.*

"Chopin, *Etudes, Op. 10, No. 3; Op. 25, Nos. 9 and 1.*

"Schubert-Liszt, '*Hark, Hark, the Lark*'; Mac-Dowell, *Witches' Dance;* Palmgren, *May Night;* Paderewski, *Polonaise, Op. 9, No. 6.*"

SIGISMOND STOJOWSKI

Mr. Stojowski writes:

"I do not minimize the importance of the subject, but many duties have delayed what otherwise would have been an eager and complete expression of opinion.

"An artist's programme is a confession of faith, and also an appeal to the public. The artist who thinks only of pleasing himself is apt to disappoint his hearers. It is easier to feel entertained by one's own performance than to hold the interest of an audience.

"On the other hand the artist who will sacrifice his own convictions in order to please an audience, betrays both his art and himself.

"Poland's greatest poet, Mickiewicz, thus expresses the function of art: 'Have a heart and look into hearts.' This means that the concept 'Art for art's sake,' should rather be, 'Art for the sake of humanity.'

"A few thoughts on programme making may be set down here.

"First. A one-composer programme, historically valuable, and, in the case of living artists, interesting, implies both a precious quality and a danger. What it contains in unity it may miss in variety. A Bach or Beethoven stands the test better than, for instance, a Scarlatti, or for that matter, a Debussy; while the two romantic masters, Schumann and Chopin, because of their rich humanity, seem ideally fitted for such use.

"Second. On the other hand, the mixed collection, which prevails at piano recitals, the 'tutti-frutti programmes,' as Anton Rubinstein rather contemptuously called them, are apt to be self-destructive through this very catholicity of choice, which often strives to include many contemporary novelties. Commendable as the search for novelty certainly is, I would prefer my colleagues to be guided by their own choice rather than by the favor or fashion of the public.

"Third. The guiding principle in programme making should be threefold, namely, respect for one's art, for one's audience and one's self. Every programme should provide some masterpieces, placed in the proper light and separated from each other by smaller canvasses, to afford relaxation to both player and listener. Aristotle's idea of 'unity in variety,' should find practical application. A programme in a single key, even with all the skill

of the performer, cannot be saved from the stigma
of monotony.   And a minor key followed by a
major of the same tonic, always seems placed in a
bad light, acoustically speaking.   From the viewpoint of what I call acoustic disposition of light and
shade, the propinquity of tonalities, in the ascending
order, is of better effect than those of the descending one.

"Fourth.   It will not do to construct a programme exclusively in the minor mode, or to have
too many minor keys in succession.   Most important
of all, the principle of 'unity in variety' must be
applied to styles.   While it is not necessary to keep
to a chronological order, a programme should not
begin with Liszt and end with Bach.   A Sonata
by Schumann or Chopin is better preceded than followed by one of Beethoven.   Contrast and similarity are the two extreme poles, between which a
programme maker must steer clear of exaggeration
in either direction.

"Fifth.   Music of the same period may provide
a better contrast than similarity of mood in greater
remoteness of time.   Thus the majesty of Bach is
better followed by the freshness and brightness of
a Scarlatti, or the serene fragrance of a Mozart,
than by the dignity and grandeur of a Beethoven.
The conventional programme, which starts with the
classics, continues with the romantics, then the
moderns and concludes with pieces in lighter vein,
has the saving grace of taking into account the

psychology of an audience, that is ready to take in, while still fresh, what is more exacting, but at the end is only able to enjoy what is easiest because of least consequence.

KATE S. CHITTENDEN

Dean of the American Institute of Applied Music, New York.

"I think that your idea is capital. I never make a programme from the standpoint of ideal classification, because I always have to consider the personal limitations of the player.

"The pupil's programme which follows is biased by two facts. It is all she can do to stretch an octave, and also she is a Barnard girl and practices an hour a day. There is always some such fact at the back of any of my arrangements. The second programme was also governed by two facts. He had a broken arm a few months ago, goes to High School, and also practices an hour a day.

"Personally, I always try to use one of the old classics, and when possible, I include something American. The Prelude, by S. P. Warren, on the first programme, is very effective, and should be known by more people.

"Programme 1, played by Margaret Spotz:

"S. P. Warren, *Prelude;* Debussy, *Les Collines d'Anacapri;* Dvorak, *On the Holy Mount;* Parsons, *Humoresque.*

"Beethoven, *Rondo, Op. 51, No. 2;* MacDowell, *Shadow Dance;* Chopin, *Nocturne, Op. 62, No. 2;* Sapellnikoff, *Danse des Elfes.*

"Brahms, *Two Intermezzi, Op. 116;* Moszkowski, *Melodie Appassionata.*

"Paderewski, *Krakoviak, Op. 9-5;* Barratt, *A Highland Lament;* Moszkowski, *Concert Valse, Op. 88.*

"Programme 2, played by Samuel Prager:

"Beethoven, *Sonata, Op. 2, No. 3.*

"Liadoff, *Prelude, Op. 42, No. 1;* Scriabine, *Prelude, Op. 16, No. 5;* MacDowell, *From an Indian Lodge;* MacDowell, *By a Meadow Brook;* Weber, *Perpetual Motion.*

"Moszkowski, *Virtuosity Etudes, Op. 72, Nos. 6, 9, 13, 2.*

"Liszt, *Love Dream, No. 3;* Bach, *Prelude and Fugue on B. A. C. H.;* Moszkowski, *Polonaise, Op. 11, No. 1.*

"(Since many of us teachers are laboring with pupils who have like limitations of time and opportunity, it is helpful to see what can be accomplished in spite of them.)"

PART V

A FEW UNUSUAL PROGRAMMES

"Old and Modern Music for Piano"

A COUPLE OF PROGRAMMES BY OSSIP GABRILOWITSCH

1. Composers of the 16th, 17th and 18th centuries:

Wm. Byrde, *Pavane, A minor.*

Couperin, *The Harvesters.*

Rameau, *Le Tambourin.*

D. Scarlatti, *Sonata, A major.*

G. F. Handel, *Harmonious Blacksmith; Allegro from 2nd Suite.*

P. E. Bach, *Rondo, B minor.*

Joseph Haydn, *Sonata, No. 2, E minor.*

Henry Purcell, *Minuet, G Major Suite.*

Daquin, *Le Coucou.*

Rossi, *Andantino, G major.*

J. S. Bach, *Prelude and Fugue, No. 22; Prelude, 2nd English Suite; Sarabande, 5th English Suite; Chromatic Fantasy and Fugue.*

W. A. Mozart, *Variations, F major; Turkish March, A major Sonata.*

2. Modern composers:

Cesar Franck, *Prelude, Chorale and Fugue.*

MacDowell, *To the Sea; Witches' Dance.*

Tschaikowsky, *Chant d'Automne; Humoresque,*
Op. 10, No. 2.

Rachmaninov, *Prelude, C-sharp minor.*

Glazunov, *Gavotte, Op. 49.*

Paderewski, *Melodie, Op. 16.*

Max Reger, *Sarabande, Op. 13, No. 7.*

Schoenberg, *Clavierstucke, Op. 19.*

Maurice Ravel, *The Fountain.*

Percy Grainger, *Shepherd's Hey.*

Edward Grieg, *Nocturne, Op. 54; Lyric Pieces,*
Op. 43.

Rubinstein, *Barcarolle, G minor; Valse, Op. 14.*

Skriabin, *Etude, Op. 42, No. 5.*

Leschetizky, *Gigue a l'Antique.*

Moszkowski, *Etude de Concert, Op. 24.*

R. Strauss, *Intermezzo, Op. 9.*

Claude Debussy, *Clair de Lune; L'Isle Joyeuse.*

Cyril Scott, *A Pierrot-Piece.*

TWO PROGRAMMES BY HAROLD BAUER

1. Piano music of by-gone times:

Froherger, *Toccata in D minor.*

Frescobaldi, *Capriccio on the Cuckoo's Cry.*

Johann Kuhnau, *Sonata in C; Combat between*
David and Goliath.

Galuppi, *Sonata, C minor.*

Couperin, *Les Barricades Mysterieuses.*

Gottlieb Muffat, *Sarabande, G minor; Fugue, G*
major.

B. Marcello, *Presto, G minor.*

Steibelt, *L'Orage.*

Hummel, *Rondo in E flat.*

Claudio Merulo, *Toccata, G major.*

Rameau, *Rondeau des Songes.*

J. C. Kittel, *Nachspiel.*

J. Mattheson, *Air Varie and Menuet.*

J. Schobert, *Minuetto and Allegro.*

John Field, *Nocturne, A major.*

2. The music of today:

Schönberg, *Clavierstucke, Op. 11, No. 1.*

Debussy, *Les Collines d'Anacapri; La Cathedrale Engloutie.*

César Franck, *Pastorale.*

Modeste Moussorgsky, *Tableaux d'une Exposition.*

Edward Royce, *Theme and Variations.*

Skriabin, *Sonata, Op. 64, 1 movement.*

Raoul Laparra, *Rhythmes Espagnols.*

Another programme of old music, played by Franz Rummel:

Wm. Byrde, *"Carman's Whistle."*

Couperin, *Le Bavolet Flottant.*

D. Scarlatti, *The Cat's Fugue.*

P. E. Bach, *Sonata, A major.*

C. H. Graun, *Gigue.*

G. F. Handel, *Suite with Harmonious Blacksmith.*

W. A. Mozart, *Gigue and Sonata with Fantasie.*

John Bull, *"The King's Hunting Jigg."*

Rameau, *Gavotte and Variations.*

J. S. Bach, *Prelude and Fugue, No. 3; Partita in B major, 6 numbers; Chromatic Fantasy and Fugue.*

J. Haydn, *Theme and Variations, F minor.*

One of the rare programmes given by Edward MacDowell, in New York:

Mozart, *Fantasie in D.*

Rameau, *The Three Hands.*

Schubert, *Impromptu.*

Grieg, *Nocturne, Op. 54.*

Templeton Strong, *Midsummer Night's Dream, Op. 36, No. 4.*

MacDowell, *Largo,* from *Sonata Tragica; March Wind; To a Wild Rose; Sonata, Eroica, Op. 50* (entire) ; *From an Indian Lodge; To a Water Lily; Elfin Dance; In Mid Ocean; Shadow Dance; The Eagle; Poem; Concert Study, Op. 36.*

A programme of modern music, by E. Robert Schmitz:

Moussorgsky, *Pictures at an Exhibition,* 8 pieces.

Debussy, *Prelude from Suite; Reflections in the Water.*

Ravel (a), *Pavanne;* (b) *Toccata.*

Albeniz, (a) *Fete in Seville;* (b) *Britana.*

Debussy, *Three Etudes from Book of Twelve Studies.*

Borodine, *Au Couvent.*
Liapounoff, *Leshinka.*

A good example of group arrangement; artist students of Mr. Carl M. Roeder:

Gluck-Saint Saens, *Alceste Caprice.*
Faure, *Impromptu in F minor.*
Paderewski, *Cracovienne Fantastique.*

Chopin, *Etude, E minor; Two Preludes, Nos. 5 and 23.*
Liszt, *Rhapsodie Hongroise, No. 10.*

Bach, *Preludium, First Partita.*
Stojowski, *Pres du Ruisseau.*
Schubert, *Impromptu·A flat, Op. 142.*
Burleigh, *Cotton Tails.*
Paderewski, *Caprice apres Scarlatti.*

Moszkowski, *Zephyr, Op. 57.*
Sternberg, *Etude de Concert, C minor.*
Liszt, *Forest Murmurs.*
Debussy, *Gardens in the Rain.*

Chopin, *Ballade, Op. 23, in G minor.*
Schumann, *Novellette in E major.*
Chopin-Liszt, *Chant Polonaise, "My Joys."*
Saint-Saens, *Etude en forme de Valse.*

PROGRAMMES BY GIFTED CHILDREN

Recital by Shura Cherkassky, Russian pianist, aged 11 (in Baltimore, 1922):

Beethoven, *"Moonlight Sonata."*

Bach, *Prelude and Bourrée.*

Correlli, *Gigue in A minor.*

Schubert, *Impromptu, Op. 90, No. 4.*

Chaminade, *Autrefois.*

Brahms, *Two Valses, Op. 39, Nos. 15 and 16.*

Mendelssohn, *Fantasie, Op. 28* (entire).

Chopin, *Prelude, D flat; Valse, D flat.*

Tschaikowsky, *Chant sans Paroles.*

Debussy, *Arabesque, E major.*

Strauss-Schuett, *"Fledermaus," Paraphrase.*

Jerome Rappaport, aged 10:

Scarlatti, *Sonata, D major; Bourrée, B minor.*

Schubert, *Impromptu in A flat, Op. 142, No. 2.*

Mendelssohn, *Songs Without Words, Nos. 12 and 45.*

Chopin, *Etude, Op. 25, No. 2.*

Grieg, *Butterfly* and *Birdling.*

Scriabine, *Prelude for Left Hand.*

MacDowell, *Witches' Dance.*

Beethoven, *Concerto No. 1, in C major,* first movement (with accompaniment).

Lenore Davis, aged five, after one year's study: *Scales and Canons* in any key (by request).

Three Five-Note Melodies; Romance, Arabesque, A Pedal Study.

Clementi, *Sonatina, No. 3.*

Bach, *Solfeggietto.*

Mendelssohn, *Consolation.*

Adams, *Doll's Lullaby,* and three little pieces about the doll, written by Lenore Davis.

Reinecke, *In the Fairy Realm; Prologue* and *The Lilliputians.*

Seeboeck, *Morning Birds.*

Rogers, *Prelude in D minor.*

Novara, *Valse a la Chopin.*

Heller, *Oberon's Horn.*

Frothingham, *The Land of Nod.*

Duo, Schulz, *Ballet Scene.*

BRIEF GLIMPSES INTO THE CLASSROOM OF THE ARTIST TEACHER

I

ALFRED CORTOT

In his own country M. Alfred Cortot is not only ranked as a consummate pianist but also as a great teacher. Not often do these two activities combine in one artist in such perfection.

When Cortot first visited America, we knew him as a pianist of the first rank, though we had proof of his ability to teach, in the playing of his gifted pupil, Magdaleine Brard. On subsequent visits to this country he has been induced to combine a certain degree of pedagogical effort with his many concert engagements.

On the evening succeeding a New York recital, on which occasion he had charmed and delighted all by the power and poetry of his performance, Cortot stepped before his class in Interpretation, held at the David Mannes School of Music.

To a foreign artist the quaint, old-world appearance of the new building housing this unique school of music, must be particularly sympathetic. The Music Saal itself, with its unadorned walls of pearl gray; its tall, many-paned windows; its one overhanging loge; its candelabra, and a pair of rich, old tapestries at either end, make it seem a part of some old, medieval castle.

M. Cortot seated himself in front of the platform, before the waiting class, and the young lady who was to interpret for him placed herself at his side. He asked at once, in French, who is to begin? A sweet-faced young player stepped upon the platform and plunged at once into the *Sonata in A major,* by Scarlatti.

Scarlatti

"Explain a Sonata," he requested.

"A classical composition in three movements," she answered.

"Non, non," he said, meaning the answer did not quite give the idea of the old music. Then he went on to explain that these compositions in earlier times were really collections of dance rhythms, which were not yet dignified by the name sonata. They were usually toccatas or suites. All the pieces were, at that time, of a popular character, in which rhythm was the most important factor. He then went to the second piano and illustrated his meaning by playing parts of the sonata under consideration. Light touch was recommended, very rhythmic and well articulated, with well-marked bass.

The next player offered Scarlatti's *Sonata in G major,* which received the artist's approval, though he showed where there might be more lightness, with half staccato touch and very flexible arms. Scarlatti, he explained, spent some years at the Spanish Court and his music is tinged with characteristic Spanish jollity and gaiety. Crossing hands imitates the guitar, also rolled chords, of which the top note should not be held.

Cortot now played a *Melodie* of Vivaldi, with exquisite variety of tone and color, differentiating the various voices. "In this kind of music," he remarked, "the melody should not be *over*-expressive, lest the other parts be obscured; all should be played simply."

The *Pastorale* of Scarlatti was recommended to be played simply and lightly. Cortot, by moving his arms, indicated the idea of floating.

Rameau

In this symposium of old music, which proved the topic of the evening, Cortot asked for an example of Rameau. A youthful pianist brought forward the *Gavotte and Variations*. The theme he found too slow and serious, advising more lightness and movement, preserving the character of the Gavotte. At the fourth Variation, where hands are crossed, the foundation note in left hand should be accented, the others lighter.

The master now contrasted early French and Italian music, saying the French aimed at a definite, specific effect, more than did the Italians. The

French have continued faithful to this early idea of illustrative titles, even down to Debussy.

Couperin's *"Call of the Birds"* was now played. Cortot wittily remarked that if there are the same kind of birds in America as there are in France, the piece pictured the twilight hour, when the birds begin calling to each other. The piece should be played with sudden shades of tone, from loud to soft, illustrating the call and answer.

In contrast to these two schools, the English with their virginal had made little progress in development at that time, for Calvinism shut down on musical expression.

Bach

Philip Emmanuel Bach has been called the father of modern piano playing. He developed the sonata form by using different themes for the second part, whereas Scarlatti had only contrasted keys, with little or no development. In Germany the church was the means of developing music. Germany used the organ principally, on which music of a more serious style must be used, rather than that of a popular or lively character. Up to Sebastian Bach's time the thumb was not used on organ or harpsichord, only the four fingers. He brought the hand up in arched position. We may say modern technic began with Sebastian Bach. He was a great student of the music of other countries as well as of his own.

A *Courante* of Bach was now played. "What kind of expression is called for in this little piece?" demanded Cortot. He answered by saying he thought it denoted quietness and happiness, indicated by light, graceful touch. Do not forget there is both a rhythmic and harmonic side to Bach's music.

"What is the origin of a ritard at the close of a Bach organ composition?" asked Cortot. He then explained that the German organs were clumsy affairs in those days. As most of the pieces ended with a crescendo, more effort was required to make this effect, therefore a ritard was necessary to produce the desired forte.

Several Bach selections were now played, a noteworthy one being the *B-flat minor Prelude and Fugue,* from Book 1, "Well-Tempered Clavichord." Cortot repeated the Prelude after the student, giving the idea of a great cathedral filled with supplicating worshippers. His performance was illuminating, fully carrying out the idea he suggested. Another Bach number was *"The Departure of a Brother,"* in which both humor and pathos are to be expressed. The player was permitted to continue to the end without interruption. Then Cortot took her place, explaining that the theme should be much slower and more expressive, and then illustrated it for the class. He puts life into Bach and into all the old music, by variety of touch and tone, and by contrasting and coloring themes.

An example of Haydn was called for and the *Sonata in D* was offered. Haydn, the master explained, lacked the depth and feeling of Bach. He possessed a certain wit and gaiety, but at the same time a certain formalism. Not till we come down to Beethoven, do we again meet the depth and richness of Bach. Haydn was a Bohemian peasant and used characteristic gypsy rhythms.

"Has anyone a Mozart example?" questioned Cortot. The larger *Fantasie in D minor* was offered. The French pianist illustrated both the Haydn and Mozart in parts, his lightness, clarity of articulation, and decisive rhythms giving them life and vitality.

Beethoven

The music of Beethoven was the theme of the next class meeting. The *Andante Favori in F major* opened the programme. Cortot in this, as in everything taken up, wishes much shading and tone color, and great attention to dynamics. "We can find all instruments of the orchestra in this composition. Let us orchestrate it then. When there are constantly changing harmonies the tempo can be slightly reduced."

The so-called *"Moonlight Sonata"* next received a hearing, and was played through without interruption. Then Cortot took the student's seat at the piano,—played the first and second movements and illustrated the third. He reminded the class that the word "Moonlight" was merely a fanciful title. The Sonata was written at a time when Beethoven was passionately in love with Julia Guicciardi. The second movement is a "flower between two abysses" —between the hopeless sadness and unutterable longing of the first part and the rage, passion, and despair of the third part, in which he rebels against fate, when he learns that the object of his passion is the wife of another. Cortot's reading of the slow movement brought out all the voices in both bass and treble—all the heart-rending wail of the music.

The second movement is cheerful, almost happy; above all, not to be hurried as some play it. It is "spoken happiness." The last movement, which he illustrated in part, was passionate in the extreme; those upward gusts of *crescendo* on the first page had accents on each beat, with a crash at the end, like an orchestra. The passages in eighths wept and wailed with sorrow and disappointment. The effect was magnificent.

The *Sonata Appassionata*, which followed, was inspired, he said, by a reading of Shakespeare's "Tempest." After it had been played, Cortot illustrated in part. The first movement needs great contrasts of light and shade. The second movement was termed a kind of religous march.

The *Sonata, Op. 81a, "Adieu, Absence and Return,"* was, like Bach's *"Departure of a Beloved Brother,"* written to depict the leave-taking of a friend.

The mighty *Sonata, Op. 106,* had the first movement offered. It was played by a man who had only worked four hours on it. Cortot listened attentively, saying that, while the other sonatas already considered portrayed in a sense personal feeling, here the master interprets humanity. He then seated himself at the instrument and went through the whole movement, delivering it with tragic intensity. In his hands it was a battle; whole armies met in mortal combat; his fingers seemed tipped with fire.

After finishing this movement, and without rising, he began the *Sonata, Op. 110,* and played it entire, saying that in all piano literature he knew of no greater example of the complete sonata— complete in melody, harmony, double counterpoint and fugue.

The class was recommended to prepare pieces by Schubert, Mendelssohn and Weber. Examples suggested were: Schubert, *Wanderer Fantasie* and *Impromptu in B flat;* Mendelssohn, *Songs without Words, Rondo Capriccioso* and *Variations,* also the *Perpetual Motion Rondo* of Weber.

This is but a glimpse of the workshop of the French master, in which he labored to impress ideas of effective interpretation in the minds of the young players before him. He constantly stressed the thought of bringing out the various voices, of creating perspective in tone, color and atmosphere, of playing with true musical feeling and inspiration.

II

Mr. E. Robert Schmitz, who so quickly sprang into prominence on his first visit to America, through his remarkable piano playing and his interesting lectures on French music, held a series of "Master Classes" the following year at the American Institute of Applied Music, which were of great value to pianists and teachers. Mr. Schmitz, who is a Frenchman to the core, was a personal friend of Debussy, and studied everything that master ever wrote, at the fountainhead. He is an eminent authority on French piano music, and on the compositions of Debussy in particular.

Mr. Schmitz, at work in the classroom, is an absorbing personality. Alert, serious, resourceful, knowing every composition from memory, able to take it up at any point, to demonstrate both as to technic and interpretation, how it should be played, proves himself an inspiring teacher.

At the outset the class was reminded that piano technic for French music was quite different from that built on German methods, "which most of us have been brought up on." Instead of the strict legato touch and sonorous, somewhat heavy style required for German music, we need to have the lightness and delicacy, the *leggiero,* the detachment of keys, the shadowy quality of tone, made by "slapping the keys," as the pianist terms it. His own playing is full of nuance, light and shade, with much variety of touch and tone. He expects young players to exhibit like qualities, though graciously lenient if they are not at once able to follow his suggestions.

Naturally only French music was taken up, principally pieces by Debussy and Ravel. At the first meeting, Debussy's *Delphic Dances* and *Jardin sous la pluie* were played, also *Jeu d'eaux* by Ravel. The Dances were inspired by a piece of Greek sculpture; the themes must be brought out by a concentration of will in the melodic finger, which declaims the melody. This finger must at times be held stiffly, without any spring, while other fingers play lightly. Prepare the fingers for chords by taking the form of the chord in the air before descending. In modern music there is a great deal of perspective; we must realize this fact when playing it.

The two "water pieces," *Jardin sous la pluie* and *Jeu d'eaux* were then discussed. The depicting of water effects is rather a favorite device with French composers. There are various sorts of these water effects. Sometimes it is fanciful water, again romantic water. Or it may be so mechanical that it seems the water must be sent through tubes, as in the Ravel piece. With the *Gardens in the Rain* you must not make it wet all at once. It must begin

gently, with drops, and a touch very soft and light,
—detached. Then by degrees the rain falls more
heavily. For the light touch, Mr. Schmitz illustrated with quiet hand, straightened fingers and
light action. Only use pedal enough to bring out
the theme. As everything gets wet, the water is in
one sheet, then all is "full water!"

One must not play piano as a baby watches his
steps. One must drive over stock and stone without picking one's way.

"You must work your material as the sculptor
molds his clay. Different sounds can be brought
out of the piano by different positions of finger and
hand. When you can do these things you become
an interpreter instead of a player."

At the second meeting, two parts of the *Suite
Bergamesque* were studied. The beautiful *Prelude*
came first. The pianist dwelt on the importance of
movement in piano playing, since it has so much to
do with the quality of tone; light, undulating movement for *leggiero*—wide, big dramatic movements
for power. "I have no more power than you," he
told the student, "but by the movements I make,
my tones seem much more powerful and ringing."
The word Bergamesque means Masque; in this
case a masque for "the whole figure," in other
words, a camouflage, a poetic disguise.

"You play the Prelude too monotonously," he
told the student. "The first page needs much
variety, and should be slower. Chords firm every

time they appear. Running passages supple, with shading. Sometimes one needs to use a light, slappy touch, with little color, like a delicate aquarelle. Octaves in bass are to be detached.

"In second measure passage, make a curve of your hand, with undulating movement. So that if I were deaf I could know, by the movement of your arm, what you were playing. You see this is not classical music; it is romantic, somewhat in the style of Massenet. By the way, never break chords, there is no expression in that; in fact it's the worst thing you can do." (No doubt there are cases where it is allowable and in good taste.) If you play very softly, make the touch merely with the weight of finger acting at the knuckle joint, but straightened.

The *Menuet,* second number of the *Suite,* was explained and played. Later came first part of the Ravel *Sonatine.* For this the slapping touch was recommended. With balanced hand, slap the melody more than the accompaniment. Shake the hand from side to side, often using just the weight of the finger.

Mr. Schmitz played this movement and added to it the *Minstrels* by Debussy.

The third meeting opened with a rendition of the charming *Ballade* of Debussy. Lacks color and movement, was the comment. For more body of tone lift your arms higher before descending; your accompaniments lack air. Lift hands off between phrases; you lack atmosphere. Don't begin too

loud. First appearance of the melody very equal—
as a straight line—quiet. After this an ever-in-
creasing crescendo. For the light passages use
slapping touch; for chord passages prepare fingers
beforehand. In soft passages touch the keys as
though touching something very delicate. In chords
the quality of tone is different when the hand is
flat from that secured when the hand is arched. In
Bach one must hold melody notes, for it is polyphonic music; in Debussy one can bring out the
melody through pedalling, after releasing the keys,
since there are not several themes going at once,
but one only. Study slapping touch with no pedal.
The slapping touch gives variety and color.

The *Menuet* from the Ravel *Sonatine* was played.
It was thought by the artist to be too stiff; it needed
more arm movement. "This Menuet is a dance,"
he said. "The dancers give rhythm but no regular
figure. Left hand begins by preparing a background for the melody above it. When you have
a weak note to play, use the fourth finger. The
last two lines have the dematerialization of the
theme; in the final *crescendo* of the last four measures use all sources of resonance."

The final number was a Chaminade *Etude*.

The fourth meeting began with Debussy's *Danse
de Puck*. "This piece must be full of atmosphere,
full of an airy lightness, which has nothing in common with the floor, or earth under our feet. Theme
in left hand we pronounced in trumpet tones; left

hand should be very staccato, each note separated with arm and hand movement. Trills here made with light arm movement, using fingers 1—4 in right hand for the *pp* trills. For light *leggiero* passages the fingers may be supple as well as the wrist. Naturally the fingers should be held close to keys in very soft playing." Mr. Schmitz now played the whole piece, giving it the necessary sprite-like character.

The last movement of the Ravel *Sonatine* was next heard, "one of the most difficult technical pieces I know of," said the artist. "In the first three measures play with both hands, not with one. Remember the thumb is heaviest; next to it the third. In seeking a fingering, consider whether force or lightness is needed. If force, use strongest fingers. Thumb lifted high for a quick, brilliant stroke can have a great power."

The class was concluded by a remarkable performance of Debussy's *Fireworks,* the last number in the second volume of Preludes. "At the beginning," he said, "we need but little noise. *Glissando* can be made with the thumb. At the explosive parts we need strong accents, made with rigid fingers. After this the piano weeps, or rather the skyrockets weep, in *white* chords, with colorless tone and absence of feeling."

The fifth morning began with a recitation of the *Briesses,* by Florent Schmitt, a light, dainty trifle. It was suggested to attack the melody note prefacing each group of four, by throwing the hand lightly with its own weight, on the key—"slapping." This will be a natural movement and should be entirely without stiffness. "If you want lightness, don't move your shoulders, nor allow any body weight to be thrown on the hands." Op. 27, No. 6, and Op. 29, No. 3 (Schmitt), were spoken of as good teaching pieces.

One of the class asked for a few words regarding Florent Schmitt.

"In appearance he is short, and rather ordinary, with close-cut hair and wears eyeglasses. His music is not purely French, but leans toward German ideas. He was a schoolteacher at first and took up music later. He seems fond of the *Viennese Valse* and has written several pieces in Viennese style. He is a fine musician, particularly in his larger works. I feel Stravinsky is above us all. Schmitt would like to be at the top, but finding Stravinsky greater, declares he will write no more."

Cesar Franck's *Slow Dance* was next rendered, a short piece of two pages, but expressive and full of color. "There should be much difference between the melody and the accompanying parts. Play it simply, in the spirit of dancing. Bring out melody in left hand, making right hand staccato with arm movement and without expression. One hand expresses life, the other nothingness, or death.

The next number discussed was the fine *Prelude* of Debussy, from the *Suite Pour le Piano*. This stirring Prelude has been compared to Bach. It certainly is romantic music; but then we know Bach was fifty per cent. romantic in his music. Of course, in Debussy, the harmony is absolutely modern. The Prelude was analyzed for touch, tone and interpretation; then Mr. Schmitz played it with entire insight into its meaning and with great variety of tonal color.

The class closed with a performance by the artist, of the series of fanciful pieces comprising *Children's Corner,* which the composer wrote for his own children.

The first number of the set, *Dr. Gradus,* is a bit of fun, poked at the technicians, Czerny and Clementi. It will be remembered that Czerny was considered a Philistine by Schumann. Play the piece *leggiero* throughout, not legato but rather slapping touch, and entirely loose arms. No. 2, *Jumbo's Lullaby,* light, slow, soft. Occasional melody notes made by slapping the full-length finger on the key. No. 3, *Serenade of the Doll,* dainty and light. No. 4, *The Snow Is Dancing,* light and delicate. No. 5, *Little Shepherd,* light, dreamy, with contrasts of light and shade on second page. No. 6, *Golliwogg's Cake Walk.* This is perhaps the most stirring of all, a little piece full of the liveliest contrasts of loud and soft; indeed a jolly jest and full of wit.

In the *Golliwogg's Cake Walk,* by the French composer, it was advised to take the descending theme with sharp accents; if single fingers are not firm enough, take several together. The big chord in bass, after the theme is announced, is to be played with that sort of relaxed body weight whose impact pushes the body backward. Further on, a high octave is taken on the rebound, so to say, and pulled off with great vigor. The softer passages following are to be played with light, rebounding, "slapping touch," which is recommended for all light, airy passages. Soft chords can be taken with slow motion. Don't try to make too much and you will make more. Soft passages with minimum motion seem shaken out of your sleeve.

For melody use the whole side of the thumb. For expressive passages incline the body somewhat forward, to add something of its weight to that of the hands and arms. "Do not play this roguish passage too nicely," cautioned the artist; "let it be a little more snappy." Big, *fortissimo* chords should be played with sweep of whole arm, with maximum weight, then bounce off.

The sixth class started with a rendition of Debussy's *Clair de lune,* played by a young teacher. It first went through without interruption, then was repeated for criticism.

"We can make many effects in this piece, by variety of touch. The whole idea is of atmosphere, of delicate aquarelle tints. Do not play it fast; rather it should be slow and dreamy. Many passages should be detached, others played with legato touch; often both are used at the same time. When you have an interval containing a black and white key, touch both before depressing them; only so will you succeed in sounding them together. My fingers must be full of *will*, there must be no flopping; hand and arm must be in one piece. On fourth page those octaves are *pure air*, taking fingers off and holding with pedal. The accompaniment is a smooth legato, 'no holes.' Make everything creepingly connected and smooth—that is where legato is necessary. Yet everything must be free and supple. *'Don't be tied to your keyboard!'* "

We next listened to the Prelude from Cesar Franck's *Prelude, Chorale and Fugue.*

"Bring out the theme through a tap or slap on the key; the accompaniment can be in the same touch, only lighter, more superficial. The interpretation should be perfectly free, like an improvisation. The poignant theme, on second page, gives the idea of something suffering, which amounts to an appeal. Later on, this appeal, which has been repeated and repeated, is at last exhausted; it has no more strength. It must now begin again, from the beginning. The work cannot be reduced to material terms of metronomic preciseness; it is full of emotion; many and varied feelings are struggling for expression. Your soul must speak through your fingers."

For the final class the compositions chosen were: Debussy, *La fille aux cheveaux de lin, Reflets dans l'eau;* Cesar Franck, *Chorale,* and both the Debussy Arabesques.

"Control the tone. Sometimes the weight of hand is too much. Chords must be homogeneous— of one sound. Don't be tied to your piano; you must often part with your piano (let go!). Lift your hands off; if the finger leaves the key, with pedal down, the string is left free to vibrate with life and vitality.

"The atmosphere of a piece depends very much on your choice of fingers to bring out the themes. Some fingers are short, others longer; some are weak, some naturally stronger. Therefore you must make a wise choice." He then played all the pieces under discussion, closing with the two Arabesques. Of the first he said it was in the nature of a free-hand drawing, and should have a free interpretation. The one in G major was more rhythmical and needed crisp accents.